A Capital Lifestyles Book, a series that offers ideas
for decorating your home and your garden
and entertaining your friends with style. Other titles include:

Blackberry Cove Herbal: Healing with Common Herbs by Linda Ours Rago

*The Gardener's Book of Charts, Tables, and Lists:
A Complete Gardening Guide* by Nancy Ballek MacKinnon

The Lunar Garden: Planting by the Moon Phases by E.A. Crawford

*Best Dressed Southern Salads: 101 Sumptuous Southern Salads
from Key West to Washington, D.C.* by Vicky Moon

An All the Year Garden by Margery Fish

Cottage Garden Flowers by Margery Fish

A Flower for Every Day by Margery Fish

Gardening in the Shade by Margery Fish

Japanese Lanterns, Elaine Husband, watercolor

Gathering in the Garden

RECIPES & IDEAS FOR GARDEN PARTIES

shelley snow & elaine husband

A Capital Lifestyles Book

Capital Books, Inc.
Sterling, Virginia

Copyright © 2003 by Shelley Snow
and Elaine Husband

All rights reserved. No part of this book may be reproduced or utilized in any form or by any means, electronic or mechanical, including photocopying, recording, or by any information storage and retrieval system, without permission in writing from the publisher. Inquiries should be addressed to:

Capital Books, Inc.
P.O. Box 605
Herndon, Virginia 20172-0605

ISBN 1-892123-93-2   (alk.paper)

Library of Congress
Cataloging-in-Publication Data
Snow, Shelley.
  Gathering in the garden : recipes and ideas for garden parties/Shelley Snow and Elaine Husband.-- 1st ed.
      p. cm.
   ISBN 1-892123-93-2
   1. Entertaining. 2. Cookery. 3. Menus. I. Husband, Elaine. II. Title.

TX731 .S56 2003
642'.4--dc21

                        2002067648

Printed in China

First Edition
10 9 8 7 6 5 4 3 2 1

This book is dedicated to our mothers,
Ruth Rogers Fowlkes
and
Helen Hawes Hudgins.
Thank you for giving us the freedom to discover who we were
and encouraging us to follow our hearts.

Hydrangeas and Pears, Shelley Snow, watercolor

The Rose Bowl, Shelley Snow, watercolor

Acknowledgments

To Phil, Elaine's husband and our rock, for teaching us how to turn on the computer and for being so selfless.

To Barry Nugent, Elaine's son-in-law, for rebuilding the computer when it blew up and getting it back to us overnight from California. We owe you more than we can say.

To John Snow, Shelley's son, for always looking out for us and believing in us.

To Betty Boner, Shelley's sister, our attorney, and our friend, we thank you.

To Debbie Fine, our agent, for finding a publisher who said yes.

Wheelbarrow with Lilacs, Elaine Husband, watercolor

Contents

10 INTRODUCTION

13 CHAPTER ONE The Tomato Taste-Off
A Coronation of the Queen of the Garden

25 CHAPTER TWO The Indoor-Outdoor Picnic
A May Rain Affair

35 CHAPTER THREE Sunrise Service
A Breakfast to Share the Morning's Glories

43 CHAPTER FOUR Café en Plein Air
A Market Buffet with the Flavor of France

53 CHAPTER FIVE A Covered Dish Country Supper
A Feast of Summer's Stars

63 CHAPTER SIX Art in the Dark
A Creative Approach to a Cocktail Supper

TABLE OF CONTENTS

75	CHAPTER SEVEN Tea Time	
	A Treasured Tradition in the Garden	
85	CHAPTER EIGHT The Unexpected for the Expecting	
	A Surprising Baby Shower	
97	CHAPTER NINE A Little Twilight Magic	
	A Dinner Party Honoring the Bride and Groom	
107	CHAPTER TEN An Angel Luncheon	
	A Heavenly Luncheon for the Special Angels in Your Life	
119	CHAPTER ELEVEN Fit to Eat	
	Low Fat, High Fun	
127	CHAPTER TWELVE Top of the Hill Birthday	
	Celebrating the Best That Is Yet to Be	
138	INDEX	

Green Fruit Salad, Elaine Husband, acrylic

Introduction

Little did we know when we met in Miss Copas's kindergarten that fifty years later we would still be sharing the friendship that was sealed instantly on that fall day. Even at five years old we saw reflections of our souls and spirits in each other.

Living on a farm and in a safe, small-town neighborhood, we were blessed with the freedom to explore and share opportunities that are rare for children today. We grabbed every minute of daylight to spend all the time we could outside. We put our name on every day, and no day was ordinary. We can still remember how it felt to realize we could spend the whole day outside. How glorious it felt just to *be*. Every season was ours to make the most of. Every day opened up new doors to leap through. Our imaginations created the world in which we lived, and we needed no props to make it happen.

This book is a compilation of shared passions developed early in life. From the time we were seven, we studied painting under the same artist and teacher. That love of art, combined with our love of the outdoors, our love of the garden's bounty and its preparation and presentation, is what this book is about. The ideas we have included for our garden gatherings are simply fun ways to take an ordinary occasion and make it extraordinary. The little stories and anecdotes that follow each chapter are glimpses into our past as best friends.

We don't profess to be expert chefs or party planners, but we do know that with a little time and imagination, you can put good friends and good food together for a memorable gathering. As you read this book, we hope you will take the time to savor the artwork, and take delight in the menus, recipes, and homegrown ideas. Recipes with an asterisk are included in full in the book.

The Garden's Bounty,
Shelley Snow, watercolor

CHAPTER ONE
The Tomato Taste-Off
A Coronation of the Queen of the Garden

For those of us who are not ashamed to admit we belong to a sacred garden club whose members are known as "tomatophiles," nothing compares to the long-awaited arrival of the Queen of the Garden. She is the one divine compensation for the long, sweaty travails of gardening in southern heat. For months we have suffered the insult of dishonest marketers who display signs touting "Home Grown Tomatoes" over mealy, tasteless objects in our produce departments. So, when the real thing comes along, we junkies have to cram into three months what we have waited for the whole year. We slice her, we stack her, we juice her, we fry her, pickle her, bake her, and best of all, slather her with mayonnaise, salt, and pepper, and sandwich her!

For a unique summer gathering, plan a coronation for the queen—a celebration that heralds her short-lived reign, highlighting a luscious, red ripe collection of recipes that glorify and epitomize the very essence of summer's heart and soul—the tomato!

Tomatoes on the Vine, Shelley Snow, watercolor

Guests are invited to bring their favorite tomato recipe for everyone else to sample. Here are some of our favorites:

*Tomato Green Chili Dip
*Cheesy Tomato Melts
*Fried Green Tomatoes
*Grilled Vegetables with Tomatoes
*Basil Tomato Tart
*Baked Tomato Casserole
*Classic Tomato Sandwiches

These tomato recipes would be great with:

*Grilled rib-eye steaks, buttered hot biscuits,
and sweet iced tea with fresh mint.*

Tomato Taste-off Special Effects

Since this party is probably one you have never had or attended, here are a few ideas to make it memorable enough to become an annual summer event for your "tomatophile" friends:

For the centerpiece on the buffet table, group together different sizes of cans of tomato products that have labels showing big, ripe, red tomatoes.

They can be empty and used as vases for summer flowers, or unopened and stacked in an interesting way in the center of the food table. Assorted sizes will make it more attractive. Place candles on top of the cans for a candelabra effect.

Summer is in full swing, so use bright summer-colored tablecloths and napkins. Mix and match your patterns using florals with checks and stripes . . . anything goes!

Glue place cards to toothpicks and stick them in a cherry tomato to be put beside each place setting.

Have all your guests bring copies of the recipe they brought to sample for the other guests to take home in a folder provided by the hostess. A table could be set up with crayons and markers for children to decorate the folder covers.

Let your guests be official judges of the recipes. Number each recipe on the buffet and have a corresponding scorecard beside each place setting. Each guest circles the number of his or her favorite tomato dish, and the one with the most votes win the grand prize. Maybe Immodium would be a welcome and appropriate prize.

Or, have "the biggest tomato" contest with a state fair blue ribbon.

String red Christmas lights in your plants or bushes for a red-ripe ambience!

If you have a scarecrow in your garden, dress her up like a real dish, and call her "Whatta Tomato."

recipes

Tomato Green Chili Dip

3 medium tomatoes, chopped
4 green onions with tops, chopped
1 small can chopped green chilies, drained
1 ripe avocado, chopped
1 small cucumber, peeled and chopped
1 small can sliced black olives, drained
1 package (2 cups) shredded Monterey Jack cheese
½ cup favorite Italian dressing

Layer first 6 ingredients, top with the cheese, and pour the dressing over all. Refrigerate at least 2 hours before serving. Serve with tortilla chips.

Cheesy Tomato Melts

1 (16-ounce) loaf of garlic bread, split
2 tablespoons real mayonnaise
½ cup basil, chopped
3 medium tomatoes, sliced
1 pound bacon, cooked and crumbled

Mr. Hunter's Tomato Stand, Shelley Snow, watercolor

Salt and pepper to taste
1 (8-ounce) package shredded aged, white cheddar cheese

Preheat oven to 450 degrees. Cut each half-loaf of bread into 3 pieces. Bake, cut side up, for 4 minutes. Spread with mayonnaise and sprinkle with basil. Top with tomatoes, bacon, and salt and pepper. Sprinkle with cheese and bake 2 more minutes.

Yield: 6 servings

Fried Green Tomatoes

4 green tomatoes, sliced 1/4-inch thick
2 teaspoons sugar
2 tablespoon cider vinegar
3/4 cup buttermilk
2 large egg whites
1 stack packaged buttery crackers (club crackers)
4 tablespoons flour
1/2 teaspoon salt
1/2 teaspoon cayenne pepper
2 tablespoons olive oil
2 tablespoons butter

Preheat oven to 450 degrees. Layer the tomato slices in shallow dish. Dissolve the sugar in the vinegar and pour over the tomatoes. (For more tomatoes, be sure to double the amount of vinegar and sugar.) Let stand 1 hour, then drain. Whisk together the buttermilk and egg whites. Place the crackers in a plastic bag and roll over them with a rolling pin until they are fine and powdery. Mix in the flour and shake well. Combine with salt and pepper and pour into a shallow dish. Dip the tomato slices into the buttermilk mixture, roll in the cracker crumbs to coat generously. In a large nonstick skillet heat the oil and butter until foamy. Add 4 or 5 tomato slices and cook 4 minutes each, or until the undersides are golden brown. Transfer the slices to a greased baking sheet, browned side up. Cook remaining tomatoes in batches, adding extra oil and butter as needed. Bake 8 to 12 minutes in the oven until golden brown. Serve with your favorite dressing.

Yield: 6 servings

Queen of the Garden, Elaine Husband, watercolor

Grilled Vegetables with Tomatoes

1/2 pound baby carrots
1 red bell pepper, cut in large pieces
1 yellow bell pepper, cut in large pieces
2 zucchini, sliced diagonally
1 large onion, quartered and separated
1/2 cup fresh Parmesan cheese
4 medium tomatoes, cut in wedges
2 tablespoons olive oil
1/3 cup balsamic vinegar
1 1/2 teaspoons molasses
1 clove garlic, minced
1/2 teaspoon salt
1/4 teaspoon pepper

Prepare the vegetables as directed. Stir together the last 6 ingredients in a large bowl. Add the vegetables and let stand 1 hour. Drain the vegetables, reserving the dressing mixture. Place all of the vegetables, except the tomatoes, in a wire grilling basket and grill over medium heat until slightly charred. Toss with remaining dressing and tomatoes and sprinkle with Parmesan cheese.

Basil Tomato Tart

1/2 cup flour
Salt and pepper to taste
1 large or 2 medium ripe tomatoes, sliced 1/4-inch thick
1 frozen pie crust
3 green onions with tops, chopped
1/3 cup fresh basil, coarsely chopped
1/2 cup real mayonnaise
2 cups grated Swiss cheese
8–10 black olives
8–10 basil leaves

Preheat oven to 350 degrees. Pour flour, salt, and pepper into a plastic bag. Place sliced tomatoes in the bag and shake well to coat. Layer tomatoes on bottom of piecrust. Top with the green onions and basil. Mix the mayonnaise and Swiss cheese together and spread it on top. Bake for approximately 35 to 40 minutes, or until cheese is bubbly and golden brown. Let stand for 10 minutes before serving. Garnish each slice with a basil leaf and an olive. This is delicious warm or cold.

Yield: 8 to 10 servings

Baked Tomato Casserole

5–6 medium ripe tomatoes,
   sliced 1/4-inch thick
3–4 tablespoons butter
1/3 cup each, chopped red
   and green bell pepper
1/2 cup sweet onion, chopped
3/4 cup herbed dry bread crumbs
1/3 cup Parmesan cheese
Salt and pepper to taste

Preheat oven to 350 degrees. Melt the butter in a skillet; add the onion and peppers and cook just until tender. (Do not overcook.) Meanwhile, in a small bowl, combine the bread crumbs and Parmesan cheese. Remove the skillet from the heat, and add bread crumb and cheese mixture, salt, and pepper. In an oblong baking dish, place the sliced tomatoes on bottom. Top with half of the bread crumb, vegetable, and cheese mixture. Repeat with a second layer of tomatoes and the remaining bread crumb, vegetable, and cheese mixture. Bake 20 to 25 minutes.

Yield: 8 servings

Classic Tomato Sandwiches

White bread
1 very ripe, large, juicy,
   homegrown just-picked tomato
Real mayonnaise
Salt and pepper

Obviously, you know what to do with the basic ingredients. A roll of paper towel is mighty handy to catch all the juice that's going to drip off your chin and roll down your arm. Here are some of our own variations that take the simple tomato sandwich to a whole new level:

To your mayonnaise, try adding one of these:

A teaspoon of vinegar, chopped fresh dill,
   and chopped fresh basil
Lemon juice, garlic chives,
   and minced onion
Roasted red peppers with a hint
   of balsamic vinegar

With these mayonnaises, try these toppers:

Crisp bacon and baby cucumber slices
   (Kirby cucumbers are best)
Cream cheese and ripe olives
Avocado slices and melted Swiss cheese
Cold asparagus spears
   with Monterey Jack cheese
Grilled portobello mushroom
   with fresh spinach leaves

Our personal favorite in all this world is this one:

Spread butter or olive oil on a good whole wheat or whole grain bread, and put it on a baking sheet in a very low oven (200 degrees). Bake until the bread is hard and crunchy. Meanwhile, chop fresh dill and basil and fold them into real mayonnaise. Slice perfect, red, homegrown tomatoes and sprinkle them with your favorite vinegar. When the bread is ready, spread it generously with herbed mayonnaise. Top with tomatoes, leaving the sandwich open-face. It is sooooo good!

Washing Tomatoes, Shelley Snow, watercolor

Bathtubs and Barn Dirt

Everyone has a garden favorite. Ours has been and always will be tomatoes. Every spring, both our fathers planted a garden full of vegetables that provided fresh produce throughout the summer and into the fall. From the time we were six or seven years old, we would sneak out to the garden with our shaker of salt, loaf of bread and mayonnaise, pick the ripest, biggest tomatoes on the vine, and eat them while they were still warm from the sun.

There were times we were known to O.D. One particular occasion stands out because we had all the symptoms of being drunk, with the hangover to match. We think we maxed out at fourteen tomatoes apiece. It was a hot, sultry day, and we situated ourselves in the shade behind the garden shed, conveniently out of sight from anyone else who might want to enjoy a home-grown, red-ripe tomato. We started out with just two nice fat ones, never intending to eat every red, round thing in the garden, but we did. At number eight or so, we noticed we were giggling quite a bit. By number ten, we were downright hysterical. However, by number fourteen, our laughter had subsided and we were sick as dogs. We stayed that way for several days, just long enough to allow the next crop of tomatoes to turn nice and red.

Elaine's daddy had a reason for raising all these tomatoes. He made the best green tomato chow chow and green tomato pickles in the world. Always doing things in a huge way, if he was going to make pickles, he was going to make tons of them. Unable to find a pot he thought was big enough, he had the brilliant idea to use the bathtub. Now, this stuff had to sit around for days for the flavors to reach their peak. To get the full picture, you have to remember these were the "one bathroom per house" days. Even today, as adults, whenever we see or smell jars of homemade green tomato anything, we cannot help but picture that chow chow floating in that tub, and one mad Mama!

Shelley's daddy also did everything in a huge way. If he was going to grow tomatoes, he was going to grow the biggest, tallest tomato plants in the world. As it turns out, he did. He had the brilliant idea of growing his tomatoes right beside the barn, in what he called "barn dirt." He raised horses, and the barn was where they were stabled, thus, lots and lots of rich, potent "barn dirt." Remember the story of "Jack and the Beanstalk"? Well, it happened with these tomato plants. Those plants grew until they reached the roof, then the vines began growing up the pitch of the roof until the tops were out of sight. They were so amazing, in fact, that the *Tennessean* newspaper sent a reporter to get the story and take a picture. Never underestimate the power of "barn dirt."

Whatta Tomato, Shelley Snow, watercolor

We go overboard on a lot of things, but we don't make our tomato recipes in the bathtub, and we don't grow our tomatoes by the barn. We do treasure these memories of our fathers and the endearing way they had of doing things their way. They handed down much more than a recipe for canning and a recipe for cultivating the tallest tomatoes; they planted in us an ever-growing love of the garden.

CHAPTER TWO
The Indoor-Outdoor Picnic
A May Rain Affair

Planning a picnic under the stars, or your garden umbrella, on your boat, or at your beach house? The weather doesn't have to be a factor in your plans. If you're having an outdoor affair and the weather doesn't cooperate, bring it indoors—or if the weather does cooperate, bring your indoors outdoors. Either way, let the sky be your limit!

(This can all be made ahead)
*Foggy San Francisco Roll-Ups
*Balmy Black-Eyed Pea Salad
Cold Front Fried Chicken
*"Dressed to Chill" Asparagus Pie
Sun-Baked Bread with Olive Rosemary Spread
*Plum Baked Peach Tart

Bringing Indoors Out, Elaine Husband, acrylic

May Rain, Shelley Snow, watercolor

Indoor-Outdoor Special Effects

Bringing the Indoors Out: Along with your invitation, include a pretend airline ticket to a romantic destination—somewhere that has special meaning to you as a couple. Give it a secret name you and your guest know.

If you really want to go all out, put up a small party tent or drape fabric to create a tent effect. Maybe you have a gazebo, garden house, or a private tree-canopied spot you can transform into a cozy hideaway.

Lighting is important. Japanese lanterns, lit with tea candles, strings of white lights, mason jars with tea lights hung from the tree branches, an old chandelier with candles, tiki torches, etc. Or, if you have outdoor plugs or enough cords, bring your indoor lamps out.

Don't forget soft music or the sound of ocean waves, a thunderstorm, or a babbling brook.

Bring out your area rug. Haul out your loveseat along with some big pillows. Of course, you'll need a table for two. There's something about an indoor setting outdoors that creates a warm, surprisingly comfortable mood.

If you have a scarecrow in your garden, dress her up in a raincoat and call her "May Rain."

Bringing the Outdoors In: As we mentioned earlier, remember to send along the menu with the invitation, including the airline ticket to a secret destination.

Go to your local nature store and browse for tapes and CDs of nature sounds, such as crickets, birds singing, rain falling, etc.

For a picnic under the stars, you can find all kinds of inspiration, from luminescent stars to whole solar systems to stick on your ceiling.

Don't forget candles and sprays scented like woods, wildflowers, and air freshened by rain.

For a little realism, try lining up plastic ants from your door to your table.

It goes without saying that a fire in the fireplace is a must if it's chilly outside. For that sunset glow, use pink or purple strings of lights in your plants.

If your destination is the tropics, scatter seashells. To create an ocean breeze, set a fan on low in a hidden location. Make or buy flower leis and dress for the occasion in your sarong. Have a tiki torch burning outside, and hang a tropical travel poster on your door. Serve drinks in coconut shells with little paper umbrellas.

The centerpiece for this tropical holiday could be lush tropical fruit and flowers such as orchids.

Pears, Shelley Snow, watercolor

recipes

Foggy San Francisco Roll-Ups

2 cups fresh spinach, washed, drained, and chopped fine
3 whole artichoke hearts, drained and chopped fine
2 green onions with tops, chopped fine
1/3 cup real mayonnaise
1 small package (3 ounces) plain cream cheese, softened
1–2 teaspoons (to taste) ranch-style dressing mix
2 slices bacon, cooked crisp and crumbled
3 or 4 (6-inch) flour tortillas

Mix the first 7 ingredients together. Spread evenly on the tortillas and roll them up jelly roll fashion. Wrap in plastic wrap and refrigerate 2 to 4 hours. When ready to serve, cut the roll-ups into 1/2 -inch slices.

Yield: 36 slices

Balmy Black-Eyed Pea Salad

2 cups fresh black-eyed peas, cooked until tender, drained
2 medium ripe tomatoes, chopped
2 Kirby cucumbers (small pickling size is best)
1/4 cup sweet onion, chopped
1/3 cup red or yellow bell pepper, chopped
Your favorite Italian dressing or bottled vinaigrette

Mix all the ingredients together and refrigerate overnight.

Yield: 4 servings

Cold Front Fried Chicken

Use your favorite fried chicken recipe; refrigerate and serve cold.

"Dressed to Chill" Asparagus Pie

1 (9-inch) refrigerated piecrust
1½ pounds fresh asparagus, trimmed
2 tablespoons butter
¼ cup shallots, diced
1 cup Gruyere cheese
2 tablespoons Dijon mustard
1½ cups half-and-half
2 eggs
Nutmeg, for garnish
Salt and freshly ground pepper to taste

Preheat oven to 425 degrees. Prick the bottom of piecrust and fill with rice or dried beans. Bake 10–15 minutes. Lower the oven temperature to 375 degrees. Blanch the asparagus in boiling water for 30 seconds; plunge them into ice water to stop the cooking process, then drain. Coarsely chop the asparagus, reserving 9 spears for top. Saute the shallots in butter until just tender. Mix together the cheese, asparagus, and shallots and pour into the piecrust. Arrange 9 whole spears, spoke-style on top, with tips pointing outward. Whisk together mustard, half-and-half, eggs, and salt and pepper and pour over cheese mixture. Sprinkle the top with nutmeg. Bake the pie for 20 minutes or until golden brown and set. Bring it to room temperature, then refrigerate. Serve cold.

Sun-Baked Bread with Olive Rosemary Spread

Purchase a good farm-style bread. Bake and slice your bread and serve with softened butter flavored with chopped black olives and chopped fresh rosemary.

Plum Baked Peach Tart

1 cup sliced almonds
1 cup all-purpose flour
2/3 cup butter, cubed
2 tablespoons brown sugar

Preheat oven to 425 degrees. Process the almonds in a food processor until they are finely ground. Add the flour, butter, and brown sugar, and process another minute or two, until the mixture resembles cornmeal. Press this mixture into an 11-inch tart pan and chill for approximately 1 hour. Line the crust with foil, fill it with pie weights, and bake for 8 minutes. Remove the weights and foil and bake another 5 minutes.

Filling:

1 7-ounce tube almond paste, sliced
2/3 cup (5 1/3 tablespoons) butter, softened
3 eggs
7 fresh peaches, peeled and sliced
3 fresh purple plums, sliced
Damson plum preserves

Preheat oven to 375 degrees. In a food processor, process the almond paste, butter, and eggs until smooth and creamy. Pour into the baked crust and arrange peaches and plums on top. Bake for 20 minutes. Remove from the oven and spread the Damson preserves over the top of the tart. Bake for another 5 minutes. Cool before slicing. Serve with whipped cream if desired.

Yield: 8 servings

The World's Longest Word

We were eight years old and it was raining. We had three choices. We could go to the "show" and let out the lightning bugs we caught last night, or, make up a new language, or write President Eisenhower to tell him about the word we made up last week that was the longest word in the English language. We opted for writing the president. We had seen a woman win $64,000 on the TV show *The 64 Thousand Dollar Question* by spelling what they thought was the longest word in the English dictionary. The word was "antidisestablishmentarianism." Well, we made up one that was a whole lot longer. Because the president was in charge of everything in the world, we knew that once he got our letter, he would make sure that our word would be the new official longest word. It was of national importance that the country know about this word because it was for their own good. After lots and lots of thought we came up with "sontresuliminateintarianismfinitequarish." (If you would like to pronounce it as well as we did, say it like this—son-tres-u-lim-i-nate-in-tar-i-a-nism-finite-quar-ish. This is how we told the president to write it in the dictionary: sontresuliminateintarianismfinitequarish, *adj.:* describing people and stuff you don't like; *syn.:* yucky; *ant.:* describing people and stuff you do like. *See also* nauseating.

 We sent the letter, then waited and waited and waited for an answer. Every year or two we would check the dictionary under "S" for our new word, but we never found it. We thought it might have been because the president thought it was way easier just to say, "yucky!"

THE INDOOR-OUTDOOR PICNIC

Tropical Picnic, Shelley Snow, watercolor

CHAPTER THREE
Sunrise Service
A Breakfast to Share the Morning's Glories

Early morning is full of glories. Why not take this time to share a beauty no other time of the day holds? The world is just waking up. There is a freshness, a fragrance, a newness in the air, and an entirely different light that is as fleeting as a tiny hummingbird or a butterfly. To capture this time and, better yet, to share it with friends, makes this gathering even more important and memorable. You will realize how valuable it is when you make the effort. Experiencing the symphonic sounds of nature that can be heard only at this time of day is made possible by the quiet.

If you have a group of morning buddies with whom you might walk, or paint, go junking, or study the Bible together, this morning picnic would be an unaccustomed treat. Since time is so precious to everyone, we've selected menus that can be made or bought ahead, packed easily, and are delicious served at picnic temperature.

*Sunrise Eggs
*Ham and Creamy Biscuits
*Green Fruit Salad with Honey Lime Dressing
*Oatmeal Cookies
Morning Glory Orange Slushes
Hot Coffee

Morning's Glory, Elaine Husband, acrylic

Sunrise Service Special Effects

Do a little homework to ensure this gathering will be an unusually special occasion. Check out the long-range forecast to select a morning that will be truly glorious. You might want to check the time of sunrise, the high tide, or anything that might affect the ambience of your picnic.

The next, and very important thing, is your location. Pick a place that is truly beautiful or special in some way, a place that is dramatic enough to create a lasting memory. Don't limit your selection to a roadside park or a typical picnic area; as long as you can get there, let the journey to your destination be part of the fun. For example, a hilltop with a stunning view, the side of a creek with its soothing sound effects, a meadow, the woods, the beach, or even your own backyard garden.

For ease in transporting, as well as an attractive presentation, pack each breakfast in an individual basket with handles to be carried by each person. You can buy disposable, lightweight, clear plastic containers at your local grocery store that may provide all you'll need. Plastic Easter eggs are perfect to pack and transport the Sunrise Eggs.

Line each basket with a small tablecloth to be used later to sit on. Tuck in other touches that add color and love, such as a tiny vase of flowers, a personalized and decorated paper coffee cup, a small citronella candle, little soaps, makeup samples, or any little gift in a tiny box.

If your setting is near a creek, the cool water is just the right "cooler" for your drinks. If you have a scarecrow in your garden, dress her in a robe and curlers, and call her "Gloria."

Don't forget to bring along your camera to capture the moment. Besides, you wouldn't want to miss what early morning light does for a bunch of beautiful friends.

recipes

Sunrise Eggs

1 dozen eggs, hard-boiled
1/4 cup real mayonnaise
2 tablespoons chives, chopped
1 tablespoon spicy brown mustard
1 teaspoon onion, grated
3 tablespoons dill pickle, chopped fine
Salt and pepper to taste
Paprika for garnish

Place hot hard-boiled eggs under cold running water to cool. Peel the eggs and slice them lengthwise. Scoop out the yolks and put them in a bowl. Mash the yolks and add next six ingredients. Spoon the yolk mixture into the egg whites, and garnish with paprika.

Yield: 1 dozen

Variations:

Instead of mustard, chives, and pickle, add to the egg yolk mixture:

2 tablespoons chopped fresh parsley
1 tablespoon lime juice
1 tablespoon capers
1 tablespoon chopped black olives

Or, instead of mustard, chives, and pickle, try adding one of these following combinations:

Lemon juice with cayenne pepper and green chilies or salsa
Roquefort cheese and crumbled bacon
Chutney, lemon juice, and about 1/2 teaspoon curry powder or to taste

How to Pack:

Just before you leave, put 2 egg halves together to form a whole egg. Wrap each egg in clear plastic wrap and place it in plastic Easter egg.

Ham and Creamy Biscuits

2 cups all-purpose flour
2 teaspoons sugar
1 teaspoon salt
1 tablespoon baking powder
1 cup heavy cream
4 tablespoons butter, melted
Spiral-cut ham slices

Preheat oven to 425 degrees. Sift together the flour, sugar, salt, and baking powder. Add the cream and mix well to make a soft dough. Knead the dough briefly (about 1 minute) on a floured board. Roll the dough out and cut it with a biscuit cutter. Dip the biscuits in the melted butter, then place them on a baking sheet. Bake for 12 to 15 minutes. Serve with a slice of spiral-cut ham. Wrap each ham biscuit individually in parchment paper and tie it with a ribbon. Bring along marmalade, honey mustard, and softened butter to serve with the ham and biscuits.

Green Fruit Salad with Honey Lime Dressing

For each individual salad:

1 curly lettuce leaf
3 slices kiwi, peeled
1 cluster green grapes
5 scoops honeydew
4 slices green pear
4 slices green apple
2 sprigs fresh mint
1 thin slice lime
1 green maraschino cherry

Arrange the fruit on a lettuce leaf and drizzle with Honey Lime dressing.

Honey Lime Dressing

$1/2$ cup honey
$1/2$ cup lime juice

Whisk honey and lime juice together until well blended and drizzle over the fruit salad.

Oatmeal Cookies

2 sticks ($\frac{1}{2}$ pound) butter
$\frac{3}{4}$ cup brown sugar
$\frac{1}{2}$ cup granulated sugar
1 tablespoon honey
2 eggs
1 teaspoon vanilla
1 cup whole wheat flour
$\frac{1}{2}$ cup all-purpose flour
1 teaspoon baking soda
1 teaspoon cinnamon
$\frac{1}{4}$ teaspoon salt
$2\frac{1}{2}$ cups old-fashioned oats
$\frac{1}{2}$ cup dried cranberries
$\frac{1}{2}$ cup dried apples
$\frac{1}{2}$ cup chopped pecans

Preheat oven to 350 degrees. Cream the butter and sugars together until mixed well. Add the honey, eggs, and vanilla, and beat until well blended. Fold in all of the dry ingredients, including the oats, and mix thoroughly. Stir in the fruit and nuts. Drop the cookies 2 inches apart on a greased cookie sheet and bake 10 to 12 minutes.

Yield: About 4 dozen

Morning Glory Orange Slushes

At most grocery and health food stores, fresh-squeezed orange juice is available in individual pint-size plastic bottles. The night before your picnic, freeze enough individuals for your guests. Tuck a straw in your basket, and by the time you reach your destination, your juice will have thawed to a slushy consistency. Voila!

Hot Coffee

Just hot, and plenty of it; that's all.

The Gelatinous Blob

The year was 1957. Banlon sweaters were in, and they were probably the most in-vogue fashion statement one could own. Shelley had one, Elaine didn't. It was no ordinary sweater. It was a lime sherbet color you could almost taste, and it was so cool.

Walking home from school one day, Shelley and Elaine decided to go down to Henderson's Creek to work on their Tarzan hideout. As they passed Shelley's barn across the field from the creek, they opened the gate and Silver, Shelley's palomino horse, trotted over to greet them. As usual, he was full of mischievousness and endearing charm. After giving him a treat, they carefully laid their schoolbooks and the precious Banlon sweater on a tree stump, went through the gate, and headed for the creek.

Among the pile of schoolbooks was Elaine's arithmetic book. Like the sweater, it was no ordinary arithmetic book; it was a particularly significant source of anxiety. The likelihood of Elaine's understanding and appreciating fifth grade math was about as probable as Elvis singing opera. In fact, the dog had eaten her homework so many times, you wouldn't believe it.

After the girls had worked on the Tarzan hideout for several hours, a light rain began to fall. They headed back to the barn to pick up their books and sweater. They were hungry, had a big arithmetic test the next day, and were extremely worried that the Banlon sweater might get wet. Heaven forbid it should shrink!

Just as the barn came into view, they saw Silver shaking his mane and tossing his head, probably expecting another treat. Little did they know he'd already had the treat to end all treats!

Suddenly they both stopped dead in their tracks. Nothing could have prepared them for what they saw. There, in the twilight of the barnyard, Silver stood in all his glory, with one slimy, holey, lime green arm dangling from his frothy, smiling mouth. On the ground before him lay the remains of what had been his first course, the mangled, disfigured body of the Banlon. The grassy green slobber, so close in color to the limey green sherbet, had soaked into the finely woven material, creating a mucuslike, gelatinous blob not unlike lime green Jell-O slowly sliding around under its own power. It was horrible!

Beach Buddies, Elaine Husband, acrylic

Just when they thought nothing could heighten their misery, Shelley turned to Elaine, unable to speak, and pulled on her sleeve. Pointing a few feet away, to what must have been Silver's appetizer, lay another mauled victim . . . the arithmetic book. The slime-smeared cover had been completely severed from the body of the book. Anything resembling addition or subtraction had been maimed beyond recognition, multiplication tables mutilated, and forget ever catching on to long division! And the only thing Elaine could say was, "Why didn't he eat the word problems?" Forget the "dog ate my arithmetic book" excuse.

CHAPTER FOUR
Café en Plein Air
A Market Buffet with the Flavor of France

Imagine yourself and your guests strolling through an open-air French farmers' market, where your senses are flooded at every turn with the infinite bounty of earth's harvest. The aromas of fresh herbs, just baked crusty baguettes, and local cheeses in olive oil pervade the air with tantalizing pungency. The richness of the colors—ranging from white asparagus, lustrous green- and plum-colored grapes, robust red tomatoes and strawberries, golden pears, perfectly shaped green artichokes to glistening black olives—creates an artist's palette. The buckets of flowers, with their delicate shades of pink, rose, periwinkle, and violet, complete the color wheel. Sounds of clucking chickens and quacking ducks, customers haggling with vendors, cart wheels on the cobblestones, and a strolling musician in the distance, make a cacophony that adds to the lively, colorful atmosphere that is the market.

Close by is an intimate outdoor café where you can sit and take in the view of the countryside while enjoying a meal that is the epitome of simple food at its freshest.

So invite your guests to enter this garden of French flavors and take the time to linger over a celebration of food and friends. From the first course to the last, let it be a summer evening to relish the harvest.

French Market, Shelley Snow, watercolor

Menu Suggestions

Plateau des Fromages (Cheese Assortment)
Saucisson aux Herbes de Frovence (French Salami)
Pain de Campagne (Peasant Bread)
*Le Navarin d'Agneau (Spring Lamb Stew)
*Quiche d'Olives (Olive Quiche)
*Poires au Vin (Pears Poached in Wine)
*Le Dome du Fromage Frais (Dome of Fresh Cheese)
*Les Tartelettes aux Pommes (Apple Tarts)

Café en Plein Air Special Effects

The idea here is to transform your garden or backyard into a French open-air market. Line up several long tables and place brightly colored umbrellas over them to create a booth effect.

Display several appetizer cheeses on straw mats or trays, enough for one tray per table. French cheese labels from the packages can be used to identify each variety and lend an authentic market look.

Have lots of different whole loaves of bread—enough to resemble a baker's stall as well as one for each table—purchased at the bakery, in baskets. As with the cheese, label the breads.

For a great look, string a variety of hard sausages, such as salami, from the top or sides of the booth. Place some on trays as well as part of the buffet. Fill the butcher's stall with a variety of choice cuts.

The main market area—the center of your buffet—should be the largest. Here you will have wire baskets of fresh eggs; earthenware containers filled with assorted olives; and produce baskets filled with fresh vegetables such as artichokes, eggplants, tomatoes, zucchini, lettuce, purple cabbages, mushrooms, potatoes, and fresh herbs. Again, label and price the items, *en français.* Any vegetable dishes, soups, salads, or quiches can be served here.

Beautiful displays of fruit and wines could be side by side. Place straw-lined baskets here mounded with luscious-colored fruits such as strawberries, peaches, raspberries, pears, apples, apricots, melons, lemons, and juniper berries. Your fruit dishes—in this case, poached pears and apple tarts—can be served here.

Next to the fruit, have your wine station. Nestled among clusters and clusters of grapes, both hanging and in baskets, display your bottles of wine. Have several different kinds of French wines, both white and red. Display bottles need not be full; they could be saved from previous occasions.

The last stall is for flowers. Fill buckets with bouquets of flowers wrapped in cellophane. Vary the types of flowers to create a gorgeous mass of color. Guests can "purchase" the bouquets to adorn their own tables.

Set up an outdoor café nearby. Use rustic tables and chairs, mixed and unmatched. Cover your tables with colored oilcloth tablecloths. Let your trees make a canopy, or set up a tent. Each table will be furnished with a flower vase with water, olive oil, crocks of butter, balsamic vinegar, knives to slice cheeses and fruit, wine glasses, bread plates, salt and pepper, etc.

recipes

Le Navarin d'Agneau

3 pounds boneless leg of lamb
3/4 cup all-purpose flour
1/4 cup olive oil
2 tablespoons unsalted butter
1 pound new potatoes
1 pound baby carrots
3 small turnips, quartered
1/2 pound pearl onions
1/2 cup celery, coarsely chopped
5 cloves garlic, minced
Salt and pepper
1 beef bouillon cube
1/2 cup dry sherry
1/2 bunch fresh thyme
1 bay leaf
1 pound Andouille sausage, sliced
1 cup shelled baby peas
1/2 pound new whole green beans
1 cup fresh parsley, coarsely chopped

Have your butcher cut the lamb into 2-inch cubes. Dredge the lamb in the flour and coat well. In a large Dutch oven, melt the olive oil and butter over medium-high heat. Add the lamb and sear it on all sides. (Do not overcook it.) Drain off the fat. Add the potatoes, carrots, turnips, pearl onions, and celery to a Dutch oven and add enough water to cover. Add the garlic, salt, pepper, bouillon cube, and sherry. Tie stems of thyme together with bay leaf to make a bouquet garni. Bring to a boil and let boil for 8 to 10 minutes. Reduce the heat, add the sausage, and simmer for 1 hour covered, then 1 hour uncovered to thicken. Meanwhile in a saucepan, bring the baby peas and green beans to a boil. Cook just until the beans are crunchy tender. Drain at once. When the stew has finished cooking, remove it from heat and discard the bouquet garni. Add the peas, parsley, and beans; return to heat; and simmer 20-30 more minutes. Adjust salt to taste.

CAFÉ EN PLEIN AIR 47

Bread and Cheese, Shelley Snow, watercolor

Quiche d'Olives

2 tablespoons shallots, chopped
1 tablespoon unsalted butter
4 eggs
1 cup heavy cream
Freshly ground pepper
1 cup Gruyere cheese, grated
1/2 pound black nicoise olives, or any oil-cured black olives, pitted
1 (9-inch) deep-dish pie shell
1 (6-ounce) package fresh spinach, chopped fine

Preheat oven to 400 degrees. Saute the shallots in the butter until lightly browned. In a large mixing bowl, combine the eggs, cream, and pepper. Add the shallots, spinach, and cheese to the egg mixture, and pour into the pie shell. Spread black olives over top of quiche. Bake 25 to 30 minutes or until golden brown. Delicious hot or cold.

Yield: Serves 8

Poires au Vin

2 cups port
1 bottle (750 ml) strong red wine, such as pinot noir
1 cup sugar
2 cinnamon sticks
Juice plus zest of 1/2 lemon
6 whole cloves
1/2 teaspoon whole black peppercorns
12 firm Bosc pears with their stems still attached
1 jar seedless raspberry preserves

In a large saucepan, combine the port, wine, sugar, cinnamon sticks, lemon juice and zest, cloves, and peppercorns. Bring to a boil, stirring until the sugar dissolves. Turn the heat down to simmer. Meanwhile, peel the pears, making sure to leave the stems intact. Remove the core from the blossom end of pear. Place the pears into wine mixture, and return them to boiling. Turn down the heat and simmer 20 to 25 minutes, or until the pears are tender but not soft. Remove the pears from the pan and place them on a serving platter. Strain the wine mixture and return it to saucepan. Cook the liquid until it is reduced to a syrup, then set aside. Melt the raspberry preserves over low heat, and add to 1 cup of the wine mixture. Allow it to cool and thicken. Just before serving, spoon the sauce over the pears. This recipe can be made a day ahead and refrigerated overnight.

Yield: 12 servings

Le Dome du Fromage Frais

Baguette slices
Olive oil
Coarsely ground black pepper
1 log Montrachet goat cheese

Brush baguette slices with olive oil and sprinkle with pepper; then bake on low heat until crisp. Serve with cheese before dessert.

Yield: 10 to 12 servings

Les Tartelettes aux Pommes

1 1/3 cups unsalted butter, softened
1 cup sugar
1/3 cup brown sugar
6 eggs
1 1/2 cups chopped pecans
2 1/2 cups flour
6 tart apples, cored and peeled
3 tablespoons lemon juice
Apple jelly for glazing

Preheat oven to 350 degrees. In a large mixing bowl, combine butter and sugars until well blended. Add the eggs one at a time, mixing well after each addition. Fold in the nuts and flour, mixing well. Butter 12 individual tart molds, and pat some dough mixture into the bottom of each. Slice the apple thinly and divide the slices among the twelve tarts. Arrange the apple slices in a pinwheel design. Sprinkle with lemon juice. Bake the tarts for 15 to 20 minutes or until their edges are golden brown. Spread apple jelly evenly over the hot tarts. Return to the oven for 5 minutes. Cool before serving.

Yield: 12 servings

"Let's Do Downtown"

Sometimes on Saturdays, when we weren't "working the neighborhood," or playing hoboes with our lunches tied on sticks, or exploring new territories, we would "do downtown."

Downtown in the 1950s consisted of two blocks on Main Street and the square. Like all other small towns during that time, Main Street was it. It was where you bought your car, your groceries, your furniture, your clothes, your tractor, or your favorite chocolate milkshake. It was where you went to the "show," had your family photograph taken, got your hair done, picked out your wedding china, and, on Saturday, you could trade your cow for a mule or a couple of pigs.

One of our favorite pastimes was "staring at the shoulder, while speaking in a foreign language," which we used to deceive people into believing we were weird. Unfortunately, we were the ones who were deceived. They already knew we were weird.

On this particular Saturday, as we started down Main Street, we discussed that it was highly unlikely we'd find an unsuspecting store clerk who had not already been a victim of our artful tactics. We passed by Hardcastle Motors, Walker Chevrolet, and Bennett Hardware. We crossed the street to Thurman's Bi-Rite and bought dill pickles on the ruse that we were there just as customers, while we scouted out the territory. However, since everyone in there called us by name, we decided to move on. Next we came to Rose's (the dime store), where the smell of popcorn and oiled wood floors wafted out to the street. Tempting as it was, we'd already covered this ground. Bypassing the bank, we proceeded to Frank's, the newest department store. Since Frank's hadn't been open that long, our prospects of finding someone who didn't know where we were from or what language we spoke was pretty good.

We entered the door separately and scoped out the situation. One of us would linger in the shoe department, while the other would move stealthily over to the pajamas. Our cue to begin was the words, "May I help you?" At this point we would converge on the clerk and respond to the question by turning and staring at his shoulder, never at his face, and spewing forth rapid, unintelligible babble that we were convinced sounded like perfect French, Italian, or Chinese. As he would move around to try to make eye contact, we would never take our eyes off his shoulder, all the while speaking our foreign language, gesturing and motioning with our hands as if we were asking him specific questions. Then, while we thought we still had his attention, we would turn to each other, staring at each other's shoulders and continue to speak as if we were communicating perfectly. At this point, we usually began to lose it, and lose our victim as well, so we knew we had to move fast.

However, he moved faster. When we looked up, we weren't staring at his shoulder any more; we were staring at his back as he ducked into women's wear.

CHAPTER FIVE

A Covered Dish Country Supper
A Feast of Summer's Stars

Cotton Wilson from Fly, Tennessee, says "If you plant somethin' you don't like to eat, you're just wastin' your time. Ain't no use in plantin' somethin' you don't like 'cause it'll know and it'll never do as well." Sometimes, though, it will thrive for your neighbor because it's his favorite. Hence, the success of the "covered dish supper"! If you have a smaller get-together in mind and want to do it all yourself, here is a menu that includes some of summer's garden stars.

Menu Suggestions

*Roasted Corn on the Cob with Cayenne Lime Butter
*Sliced Tomatoes with Basil Onion Mayonnaise
*Warm New Potato Salad
Fresh-Cooked Green Beans
*Zucchini and Yellow Squash Casserole
Cucumber and Onions in Vinegar
*Strawberry, Peach, and Plum Shortcake

Soul Food, Elaine Husband, watercolor

Country Supper Special Effects

Here are some ideas that will give your next hoedown a down-home kind of flavor. Even if you're a suburb or city dweller, why not take your friends and family back to the day when people gathered in their backyards, not to impress each other, but for fellowship and plain fun?

For decorating the tables, here are some suggestions: Go down to your farmer's market or produce stand and talk them into giving you some of those produce baskets they usually throw away. You can do so many things with them—fill them with some yummy-colored veggies, like eggplant, yellow squash, peppers of all kinds, etc.—and place bouquets of flowers among the vegetables. Why buy them at a florist when nothing looks prettier with farm food than wildflowers?

Blue-and-white-checked tablecloths give a perfect down-home country feel. Combine them with bright yellow sunflowers for a warm, sunny effect

Use the produce baskets lined with a pretty napkin to hold all your silverware.

Nothing captures that out-in-the-country attitude like an old tire sprayed white and filled with petunias! Find a small tire, spray it, and plop it on your food table as a centerpiece. Fill it with bedding plants to plant in your yard later.

Top small dowels with seed packets stuck in potatoes and place beside the corresponding dish, or use the seed packets as place cards. Watch and see if the cool guy sits at the cucumber, the pregnant woman picks the watermelon, or the workout queen chooses the pole beans.

Use clay pots to hold dishes of condiments like your killer onion mayo and herb butters.

Create a vase by surrounding a straight-sided container with fresh carrots, tops attached, and tied with twine to hold flowers. The carrot tops make beautiful greenery to set off the colors in your arrangement.

Rig up a clothesline to display favorite summertime recipes, held in place by wooden clothespins.

If children are coming, plan ahead for their fun and let them set up an old-fashioned lemonade stand.

Fill a wheelbarrow with ice to keep drinks cold. Use a small garden spade as an ice scoop in your cooler. For a beautiful splash of color, add another wheelbarrow filled with lilacs or wildflowers.

Buy life-size plastic chickens or ducks at your local dollar store and put them down by your mailbox to let your guests know they've found the right hoedown.

As favors, give jars of homemade jelly, pickles, or chow chow. Buy inexpensive toy tractors, wagons, or pickup trucks for the kids.

If you want to go "whole hog," stencil life-size pigs, cows, and mules on plywood, have them cut out, and place them around the yard.

If you have a vegetable garden of your own, it would be the perfect setting for this shindig. Best of all, build a scarecrow, dress the old girl up as the hostess for this hoedown, and call her "Maizie."

recipes

Roasted Corn on the Cob with Cayenne Lime Butter

Hot, buttery, tender, succulent, fragrant, and delicious . . . there are no adjectives yummy enough to describe fresh summer corn. One of the best ways we know to experience the bounty of this blessing fully is to roast the ears in their husks, and serve them hot with assorted herb butters. A fun and attractive way to serve the butters is to use molds of different shapes. For this party, we suggest pouring softened butter into a cornbread stick mold, which shapes the butter into little ears of corn, and refrigerate. We inherited, or stole, our mother's cast-iron ones, but you can purchase them at hardware or cooking stores.

12 ears fresh corn
2 sticks unsalted butter, melted
Juice plus zest of 2 limes
1/2 teaspoon cayenne pepper
1/2 teaspoon salt

(For variation, add 1/4 cup of one of the following (chopped): dill, cilantro, or chives)

Peel the corn husks all the way back, but leave them attached. Rinse the cobs in cold water, and remove the silk. Soak the corn in water to cover for at least 1 hour. In a small bowl, combine the butter, lime juice and zest, pepper, and salt. Spread melted butter over the corn and smooth the husks back into place. Tie the tops together with twine. When coals are ready, grill the corn, turning often, for 20 minutes. When cool, remove twine and husks and serve with additional herb butter if desired.

Yield: 12 servings

Sliced Tomatoes with Basil Onion Mayonnaise

1 medium Vidalia onion, peeled
1 empty quart jar with lid
1 pint real mayonnaise
½ cup chopped fresh basil
10–12 homegrown tomatoes
Freshly ground pepper to taste

One week before serving, place the whole, peeled onion in the quart jar. Cover with 1 pint of mayonnaise, seal, and refrigerate. Two hours before serving, remove the onion from mayonnaise. Place the flavored mayonnaise in a serving bowl and add the chopped basil and pepper. Cover and refrigerate until ready to serve as an accompaniment to sliced tomatoes.

Warm New Potato Salad

3 pounds red new potatoes
1 pound thick-cut bacon
⅔ cup real mayonnaise
1 teaspoon salt
1½ teaspoons freshly ground pepper
½ teaspoon garlic, minced
¼ cup red wine vinegar
2 teaspoons sugar
½ cup red onion, minced
1 cup fresh parsley, chopped

Cook the unpeeled potatoes until tender. Drain and cover them with cold water. Cook the bacon until it's crisp, drain it on paper towels, and set aside. Crumble the bacon when it has cooked. Combine the next 7 ingredients in a bowl and whisk together until blended. Cut the potatoes into slices and place them in a large serving bowl. Combine them with the dressing and marinate 1 hour. Before serving, add crumbled bacon and chopped parsley.

Yield: 8 to 10 servings

Zucchini and Yellow Squash Casserole

1 pound yellow squash
1 pound zucchini squash
1 medium onion, chopped
1 cup grated cheddar cheese
1 (3-ounce) package cream cheese
2 eggs, beaten
3 tablespoons butter, melted
Salt and pepper to taste
1 stack crushed buttery crackers

Cook the sliced squash until tender, then drain it well. Meanwhile, preheat the oven to 350 degrees. Combine $\frac{1}{2}$ the cheese and the rest of the ingredients, except the crackers, and add the mixture to the squash. Pour into a greased casserole, sprinkle with the remaining cheese, top with the crushed crackers, and bake for 25 minutes.

Yield: About 8 servings

Sunflowers, Elaine Husband, acrylic

Strawberry, Peach, and Plum Shortcake

Cake:

1/3 cup butter
2 cups all-purpose flour
2 tablespoons sugar
3 teaspoons baking powder
1 teaspoon salt
3/4 cup milk
Melted butter

Preheat oven to 450 degrees. Mix the first 5 ingredients in a food processor until the mixture resembles fine crumbs. Transfer it to bowl and stir in the milk. Knead on a lightly floured cloth until smooth. Roll the dough 1/2-inch thick and cut it into 3-inch circles. Bake the circles on an ungreased baking sheet for 10 to 12 minutes. Split crosswise while they are still hot and brush both halves with butter.

Topping:

1 pint strawberries, sliced
3 ripe peaches, sliced
5 medium plums, sliced
1/2 cup sugar

Toss the sliced fruit in a bowl with the sugar and let stand.

Filling:

1 (8-ounce) package cream cheese, softened
1 cup whipping cream, chilled
1/4 cup powdered sugar
1 teaspoon vanilla extract

Beat all the ingredients until stiff peaks form. Using half of the filling, spread it on the bottom half of each cake. Using a slotted spoon, top with fruit, then use the remaining filling to spread over the fruit. Cover each cake with its top and drizzle it with the remaining fruit juice. Dust with powdered sugar and serve.

Yield: About 12 servings

The Garden

Our love of the garden today began when we were young children growing up in a rural southern town and spent our summers mostly outdoors. Our parents and everyone we knew had their own vegetable gardens, and gatherings in the backyard to share friendship and the garden's bounty were a common occurrence.

We share memories of hot, hazy late afternoons when the countryside appeared to be washed with watercolors, silhouettes of old blue cedars lined the fencerows, and lazy creeks bordered by patchwork-quilted fields of wildflowers. Sounds of screen doors slamming, the clinking and clattering of dishes coming from the open kitchen windows, katydids and crickets singing from the hedgerows, and the happy squeals of children playing were the essence of summertime and suppertime.

Daddies were grouped around the grill, and mammas carried out big bowls of sumptuously prepared vegetables straight from the garden. Sometimes the children got to chase away the wild array of poultry that strutted, clucked, and pecked too close to the food table, and after dinner the hot pursuit of lightning bugs kept us busy while our parents lingered over laughter and coffee.

Sometimes at the end of the evening, when we piled exhausted into our cars to go home, a soft rain began to fall. For us, it was part of the magic because it was like a curtain falling over the day, making the air as fragrant as peaches washed clean in the kitchen sink.

It's hard to believe our lives have been so enriched by something as simple as a garden.

Lemonade Stand, Elaine Husband, acrylic

CHAPTER SIX
Art in the Dark
A Creative Approach to a Cocktail Supper

If you're one of the countless millions who are not having a portrait unveiling or a gallery opening, why not? If you have a birthday party coming up or a gourmet supper club meeting at your home, or any occasion to entertain, "Art in the Dark" would be something entirely different and fun. The special effects of this occasion are stunning in an outdoor setting, especially if you're lucky enough to have a sunset over your garden that creates a painting itself.

Menu Suggestions

*Fruit and Vegetable Artist's Palettes (see Special Effects)
*Cezanne's Creamy Fruit Dip for Fruit Palette
*Monet's Mayonnaise for Veggie Palette
*Pissarro's Pepper Artichoke Pizza
*Degas's Dilled Cucumber Curls with Smoked Salmon Spread
Van Gogh's Green Beans and Asparagus with Vinaigrette
Toulouse's Tomato and Goat Cheese Bruschetta
Modigliani's Mount of Olives
*Gauguin's Great French Macaroons

Still Life with Hyacinths, Shelley Snow, watercolor

Art in the Dark Special Effects

When you send the invitations, give each person the name of another guest, whose portrait he or she is expected to paint. The night of the party, guests have to bring their finished portraits for the unveiling. The famous art critics, your guests, will guess who is who. Assign someone to act as a juror and give awards for each category. Be sure to have enough awards for each guest to fit into some category. For example, your categories might be "Best of Show," "Worst of Show," "Most Unrecognizable," "Most Mediocre," "Most Representational of a Human Being," "The Wettest Canvas," "The Smallest," "The Largest," etc. So your guests "get the picture" that this is all in fun, list the award categories on the invitation.

After the awards ceremony, your guests can stand around and ask each other, "What do you think the artist is trying to say here?"

It is not out of the question to have an auction, preferably a silent one, to sell the portraits. If any money is actually raised, donate it to the most deserving artist you know, or split the proceeds and all go out to a movie.

If this idea doesn't do it for you, have each guest come dressed as his or her favorite painting. For example, someone with properly placed coconuts and a sarong could be one of Gauguin's native girls. If only half of someone's mouth is smiling, surely, she's the Mona Lisa. And if a haystack walks in, well . . .

Going to the trouble to arrange the flowers and fruit we suggest here is well worth the effort because they make a gorgeous and extremely "impressionistic" display.

The Edible Fruit Centerpiece

For the base of this centerpiece, have a thin sheet of plywood cut in the shape of an artist's palette (at least 3 feet long). As if representing the colors of paint on an artist's palette, fruit and flowers of the same color should be grouped together. For example, start with yellow fruits and flowers, such as pineapple chunks, lemons, and star fruit interspersed with yellow roses. Moving around the color wheel, next use fruit and flowers in the peachy orange and apricot range. Next go to the reds with strawberries, cherries, etc., then to pink, on to purple, then to blue. Greens are next, such as honeydew, grapes, limes, and green hydrangea blossoms.

Roses and Tulips, Shelley Snow, watercolor

The Edible Vegetable Centerpiece

Using the same artist's palette idea as above, substitute chopped vegetables for the fruit. Use the flowers as well, arranging them with your vegetables in the same manner. Yellow peppers and squash mixed with yellow marigolds can get you going. If you just want a luscious-*looking* centerpiece, leave the vegetables uncut and combine them with the flower blossoms.

Make your own still lifes to resemble Old Masters' paintings and surround them with antique frames of different sizes. The drink or serving table makes an ideal setting for this display.

Artists' palettes can be used as serving trays, and miniature easels can display the menu.

Other ways of making the party more fun are to use blank paper place mats with a small box of crayons at each place setting, and place cards set on individual miniature easels. Instead of just printing guests names, go to your favorite bookstore or museum shop and purchase postcards of famous paintings. Pick out paintings ranging from Picasso to the Old Masters and write the name of the guest on the back of the postcard who most matches the personality of that artist. See how many people guess where they are supposed to sit.

If you gather in your garden, dress a scarecrow in a smock and beret, and call her "Fran Go."

Yellow Flowers, Shelley Snow, watercolor

recipes

Cezanne's Creamy Fruit Dip for Fruit Palette

2 (3-ounce) packages cream cheese, softened
2 tablespoons lemon juice
4 tablespoons red plum jam
1½ cups whipping cream

Beat all ingredients together until smooth. Chill at least 1 hour before serving. Makes approximately 2 cups.

Monet's Mayonnaise for Veggie Palette

½ cup tarragon vinegar
1 teaspoon dried tarragon
2 tablespoons chopped green onions
½ teaspoon chopped parsley
1½ cups real mayonnaise
1 teaspoon grated lemon rind
¼ teaspoon freshly ground pepper

Simmer vinegar, tarragon, onions, and parsley until reduced to approximately ⅛ cup. Let cool, then stir in the mayonnaise, lemon rind, and pepper. This can be chilled and kept up to seven days. Makes approximately 1 cup.

Pissarro's Pepper Artichoke Pizza

2 teaspoons olive oil
1 red bell pepper, cut in strips
1 orange bell pepper, cut in strips
1 medium onion, sliced thin
¼ cup real mayonnaise
2 cloves garlic, minced
¼ teaspoon crushed red pepper
1 (9-ounce) package frozen artichoke hearts, thawed
1 large Italian cheese-flavored pizza crust
½ cup feta cheese, crumbled
¼ cup fresh flat-leaf Italian parsley

Preheat oven to 450 degrees. Heat the olive oil and sauté the pepper, onion, and garlic about 4 minutes. Set aside. In a food processor, process mayonnaise, garlic, red pepper, and artichoke hearts until they are finely chopped. Place the pizza crust on a baking sheet and spread with the artichoke mixture. Top with pepper and onion mixture, feta cheese, and parsley. Bake 15 minutes or until crust is crisp. Serve cold or hot. Serves 8.

Degas's Dilled Cucumber Curls with Smoked Salmon Spread

6 medium cucumbers
4 tablespoons chopped fresh dill
2 tablespoons fresh-squeezed lemon juice
1 tablespoon sugar
2 tablespoons real mayonnaise
2 teaspoons Dijon mustard
3/4 teaspoon salt

Peel the cucumbers with a potato peeler and slice them in half. With the potato peeler, peel long, thin ribbons from each cucumber, discarding the seedy centers. Refrigerate for at least 3 hours.

Dressing:

Whisk together the remaining ingredients and pour over chilled cucumber curls.

Still Lifes, Elaine Husband, watercolor

Smoked Salmon Spread

1½ packages (8 ounces each) cream cheese, softened
¼ pound smoked salmon, chopped
3 tablespoons capers, drained
¼ cup chopped fresh dill
2 tablespoons minced onion
1 tablespoon lemon juice
Fresh parsley for garnish
Assorted crackers

In a medium bowl, mix all of the ingredients, except the parsley and crackers, until blended. To serve, sprinkle the top of the spread with parsley, serve with crackers, and top with cucumber curls. Makes about 4 dozen pieces.

Modigliani's Mount of Olives

Select several varieties of olives at your supermarket deli section. Mound them on a serving tray and surround them with an assortment of imported cheeses.

Gauguin's Great French Macaroons

4 ounces fresh coconut, shredded
1 teaspoon vanilla extract
⅛ teaspoon salt
Sweetened condensed milk
2 egg whites, stiffly beaten
Sifted confectioners' sugar

Preheat oven to 250 degrees. Combine the coconut, vanilla, and salt with enough sweetened condensed milk to make a thick paste. Fold in the egg whites. Drop the batter from a spoon onto a greased baking sheet. Bake until lightly browned and when cool, roll them in confectioners' sugar. Makes approximately 20 cookies.

The Mummy

The eighth grade science fair was coming up, and we decided our entry had to be unlike any that had ever been submitted. We adored the mystery of archaeology, especially when we made up our own mysteries, planted our own treasures, collected our own data, and came to our own conclusions. We loved "mummified stuff" as well. (We each owned a "real live" shrunken head we had ordered from the back page of a comic book.) So, we decided to build and preserve our very own mummy as our science project.

Hats, Elaine Husband, acrylic

The first step was locating a body. The Roberts' Store came to mind because the people who worked there were about a thousand years old. Everything in the store was old. Originally opened in the late 1800s, it served as our town's only dry goods store, and, even in 1959, nothing had been changed. The goods were really dry now! We were certain that if anybody had an old, old mannequin to use for a body, Roberts' surely would.

On Saturday morning, we walked down to the Roberts' Store to ask if we could have one they didn't use anymore. After a lot of explaining, the blue-haired ladies finally said to go on up to the attic and see what they had. To us, going to the attic of the Roberts' Store was like going on an archaeological dig all by ourselves. We figured we might find all kinds of stuff already mummified.

When we got up there, it was everything we had imagined. Decades of dust created a fabulous stifling gloom, and the stacks of old boxes undoubtedly were filled with relics and treasures we could stick in our own mummy's coffin for his afterlife stuff. Well, we didn't find any relics, but we did find an old dress form that had great potential.

Now that we had our "body," we had to prepare him for his burial, and we intended for it to be royal. Our first move was a trip to the town's cheese plant.

Wanting the mummy to be genuine, we took our cheesecloth through several degrees of "rottenizing." Our first step was to simmer it on the stove overnight in coffee grounds, producing a natural mummy color. (Our parents must have been out of town.) Next, way out in the backyard, we aged it further by soaking it in Dr. Pepper, a forgotten furry casserole from the fridge, and old blue cheese, generously donated to us by the cheese plant. (At this point our parents were back in town and strongly suggested we move on to step three, the burial.)

Designing a head from a cantaloupe, we wrapped the entire form, weaving our decayed cheesecloth in a pattern to look Egyptian. After a couple of spring showers, and ten days underground, we dug up—a mummy that really did look a thousand times more authentic than the one in the movies. We think the rotten cheese is what did it. And we won first place!

Portraits, Elaine Husband, acrylic

CHAPTER SEVEN
Tea Time
A Treasured Tradition in the Garden

R emember when you were little and you had tea parties with your dolls? Why not invite your most treasured friends to celebrate for no special reason except friendship? There are so many ways to make it a memorable occasion no matter what your taste, your budget, or your timetable.

Menu Suggestions

*Buttery Asparagus Roll-Ups

*Dilled Shrimp Canapés

*Roasted Pepper and Olive Canapés

*Tomato Aspic with Avocado Mayonnaise

*Cucumber Tea Sandwiches

*Cheese Straws

*Apricot Almond Tart

Tea Time, Shelley Snow, watercolor

Tea Time Special Effects

If fine china isn't your thing, or you don't have any, create your own table settings with your everyday and dress it up. For example, tie assorted colored ribbons to the handles of your cups or take tiny edible flowers such as violets, pansies, or roses, and make little bouquets to place on each plate. Baby food jars make excellent vases at each place setting.

If you have miniature tea sets, group them around the centerpiece.

Create a tea wreath for your front door. Starting with a grapevine wreath, attach miniature teacups, teapots, pretty tea strainers, little teaspoons, and tea bags. Wind ribbon through the grapevine and top the wreath with a bow.

Use gloves, fake pearls, and garden party hats as mailbox decorations or centerpieces.

Use fresh asparagus spears to encircle candleholders or vases of flowers and secure them with ribbon.

In pretty paper, wrap individual gifts for each guest that contain inexpensive treasures:

- *A variety of special teas, a tea strainer, or a pretty tea bag rest*
- *Old demitasse spoons from a local flea market*
- *Sweet little "nothings," like forget-me-not flower seeds or antique buttons*
- *Photographs of you with your friend, fragrant soaps, favorite recipes*
- *Old hat pins, sachets tied with old pieces of lace . . . basically anything that strikes a heart chord*

For a beautiful touch, make or have made small individual cakes for each place setting. Ice them to look like gift packages, making each one unique with different colored satiny bows. Write each guest's monogram in icing on the top or make a gift tag of icing with the guest's name in script. These cakes can be your dessert, or guests can take them home as party favors.

Decorate each chair with flowers tied with tulle bows or scarves, all the same or different to suit the personality of each guest.

Be creative in presenting your tea fare. Arrange all appropriate condiments on a large silver tray. For example, include violet blossoms on cubes of sugar; party toothpicks skewered with assorted lemon, lime, and orange curls; mint leaves (spearmint, pineapple, etc.); or fresh berries. Put spices into squares of tulle tied with peppermint dental floss. Be sure to use fresh flowers, doilies, ivy or violet leaves, or anything that makes this tray a feast for the eye.

If you have a scarecrow in your garden, dress her up for tea time and call her "Miss Vidalia."

Miss Vidalia, Shelley Snow, watercolor

recipes

Buttery Asparagus Roll-Ups

Fresh asparagus tips
Lemon juice
Thin bread slices
Butter, softened
Real mayonnaise

Preheat oven to 400 degrees. Place the asparagus tips in boiling water until blanched, drain them well, and drizzle them with lemon juice. Cut the crust from the bread slices and roll them out with rolling pin to flatten them. Spread one side of the bread with softened butter, then turn it over and spread the other side with mayonnaise. Place an asparagus tip on each slice, roll it up, and secure it with a toothpick. Place the sandwiches on a cookie sheet and bake until they are golden brown, approximately 5 minutes.

Dilled Shrimp Canapés

8 ounces fresh or frozen tiny shrimp, cooked and coarsely chopped
3 teaspoons fresh-squeezed lemon juice
1 1/2 tablespoons chopped fresh dill
5 teaspoons minced sweet onion
1 (3-ounce) package cream cheese, softened
2 tablespoons real mayonnaise
25–30 buttered and toasted baguette slices
Dill sprigs for garnish

In a bowl, combine all the ingredients (except the baguette slices) until well blended. Top each toast round with a teaspoon of the shrimp mixture and garnish it with a sprig of fresh dill. Place on a cookie sheet and broil for 3–4 minutes until golden.

Roasted Pepper and Olive Canapés

20 slices dark brown bread thinly cut into rounds or squares and toasted.

5–6 ounces goat cheese (such as Montrachet) or cream cheese, softened

3/4 cup kalamata olives, well drained, pitted and chopped

2 (7-ounce) jars roasted red peppers, sliced, drained, and patted dry

Spread the toast rounds with cheese, add the chopped olives, and top with the roasted peppers.

Tea Cakes, Elaine Husband, watercolor

Tomato Aspic with Avocado Mayonnaise

3 tablespoons unflavored gelatin

1/2 cup plus 1 1/2 cups low-sodium vegetable juice, chilled

2 cups bottled Bloody Mary mix

1/2 cup diced celery

1/2 cup sliced black olives

Soften the gelatin in 1/2 cup of cold vegetable juice. Mix the remaining vegetable juice and Bloody Mary mix in a saucepan and heat thoroughly. Dissolve the gelatin mixture in the hot mixture. Remove from the heat and chill until partially set. Stir in the chopped celery and olives and pour the mixture into individual molds. Chill until firm. Just before serving, unmold the aspic and top it with avocado mayonnaise.

Yield: Approximately 10 small molds

Avocado Mayonnaise

1 avocado, chopped
2 tablespoons real mayonnaise
1 tablespoon lemon juice
Salt and pepper to taste

Mix all of the ingredients until smooth and chill until ready to serve.

Cucumber Tea Sandwiches

1 (8-ounce) package cream cheese, softened
$1/2$ cup real mayonnaise
1 teaspoon garlic salt
3 teaspoons chopped fresh chives
$1^1/2$ teaspoons dried chervil
$1/4$ cup white wine vinegar
1 tablespoon sugar
8–10 small cucumbers, peeled and thinly sliced
1 loaf whole wheat or white bread, sliced thinly
Fresh dill weed for garnish

Combine the cream cheese, mayonnaise, garlic salt, chives, and chervil in a bowl, and refrigerate for at least 1 hour. Meanwhile, combine the vinegar and sugar. Place the cucumber slices on a platter and drizzle the vinegar mixture over them. Let stand about 20 minutes. Cut the bread into small rounds and spread each one with the cream cheese mixture. Drain the cucumbers and pat them dry. Top the cream cheese with a cucumber slice and a sprig of dill for garnish.

Yield: About 60 sandwiches

Cheese Straws

1 pound sharp cheddar cheese, shredded
$1^1/2$ cups all-purpose flour
$1/4$ cup butter, softened
1 teaspoon salt
$1/4$ teaspoon ground red pepper

Preheat oven to 375 degrees. In a food processor, combine all of the ingredients and process until the mixture forms a ball. On a lightly floured surface, roll out the dough ¼-inch thick and cut out rounds with a small cookie cutter. Place on an ungreased baking sheet and bake for 8–10 minutes. Cool and serve.

Yield: Approximately 3 dozen

Apricot Almond Tart

1 (9-inch) prepared piecrust
3 large eggs
¾ cup apricot preserves
¼ cup (4 tablespoons) butter, melted
¾ cup sugar
½ teaspoon almond extract
1 cup slivered almonds, toasted
½ cup dried apricots, chopped finely

Preheat oven to 450 degrees. Fill the piecrust with dried beans and bake at 450 degrees for 8–10 minutes. Set aside. Lower the oven temperature to 350 degrees. Combine the eggs, apricot preserves, melted butter, and sugar and beat with a mixer until well blended. Add the almond extract, and apricots. Pour the mixture into a prepared piecrust and cook at 350 degrees for 50–55 minutes. After 30 minutes of cooking, cover the tart loosely with foil to prevent excessive browning.

Serving suggestion: Let cool and top with fresh whipped cream flavored with 1 tablespoon amaretto.

Yield: Approximately 8 servings

Chatting on the Balcony, Shelley Snow, watercolor

Four O'Clock Tea

As young children, we invented a "Four O'Clock Tea" recipe made of crushed pink four o'clock flowers and water to serve to the fairy community. After the tea had steeped enough, we spent the rest of the day searching for and gathering what we needed to create the perfect tea party. Wild strawberries, elderberries, nuts, and seeds went into our jams and cakes. Blueberry bonbons, sugared violets, and primrose petit fours made more delectable desserts. We collected dandelion greens and watercress for our salads, with a pretend honeysuckle dressing to serve in acorn cups.

A silver thimble served as an elegant teapot, with lily of the valley blossoms making perfect tiny teacups.

The spot we chose for the party was always a secret place we believed only little people could see, such as under the cover of a dense thicket or in the hidden mossy valley between great old tree roots.

On a particularly magical day, some of our treasures would be an aqua blue robin's egg, a bright blue bird feather, or a nugget of amber-color glass glistening in the sun. Queen Anne's lace became beautiful parasols. Morning glories became trumpets, and snail shells were French horns. We were thrilled if we spotted the wing of a dragonfly or butterfly to make a kite. Tiny primroses, wild violets, and forget-me-nots made little quilts of color.

That night when we went to bed, we just knew our little guests were beginning to dance, to play, and to sit down on little thread spools for Four O'Clock Tea.

Tea Service, Elaine Husband, acrylic

CHAPTER EIGHT

The Unexpected for the Expecting
A Surprising Baby Shower

You may have a close friend or family member who "looks like she swallowed a watermelon seed." A baby shower is a joyous event that deserves to be as charming and special as you can make it. We have chosen a watermelon theme that lends a fresh twist to a party that typically is done with the same overused ideas.

Why not provide the unexpected for the expecting? From a nontraditional menu that delivers a dessert of pickles and ice cream to a load of zany special effects, this shower will be as fun for the guests as it will be for the new parents.

First Trimester (Appetizers)

*Bundles of Joy
*Watermelon Punch with Fresh Fruit Garnish

Second Trimester (Main Course)

Onesie Cornish Game Hens
*Cherry Tomato Salad with Spanked Baby Bottom Dressing on Bibb Lettuce
*Blue Cheese Tater Tots (Blue Cheese New Potatoes)
*Veggie Triplets (Broccoli Florets with Carrot and Zucchini Squash Ribbons)

Watermelon Oasis, Elaine Husband, acrylic

Third Trimester (Dessert)

*Due-Date Nut Bars
*Peachy Pink Ice Cream with Blueberries
Kosher Dill Midgets
Baby Dill Gherkins and Jumbo Olives

The Unexpected for the Expecting Special Effects

When sending the invitation, enclose a copy of the menu. Use tiny type for fun.

Bored with the baby bootie petits fours? Buy four or five long watermelons and dress them in diapers and baby bonnets on opposite ends. Put your "babies" in bassinets, baby carriages, old high chairs, or whatever baby gear you have.

For your centerpiece, carve a large watermelon into the shape of a baby carriage and fill it with watermelon punch, using cantaloupe rings for wheels.

Another lovely centerpiece idea is to use a watermelon as an oasis and flower container as well. Make holes in the watermelon to hold flower stems and greenery. You can use all pink or all blue flowers, or a lovely mixture from your garden.

Why not really "baby" your guests and serve them their drinks in baby bottles? Straws can be substituted for the bottle nipples.

Make a bib for every guest to wear at dinner. Personalize each with the guest's name or monogram.

Have each guest bring a baby picture of himself or herself, and number and display them, letting everyone guess who is whom. The one who guesses the most correctly wins a prize such as a free night of baby-sitting or one of the watermelon "babies."

Play lullabies as background music.

Pickles and Olives, Shelley Snow, watercolor

Leaving the label on the empty baby food jars, use as votive holders at each place setting.

Use cloth diapers as your "linen" napkins. Fold them like an old-fashioned diaper and secure them with a big diaper pin.

If you have a bar set up, make a sign that reads, "Epidurals Served Here."

For party favors, place a jar of homemade pickles tied with pink or blue ribbons at each guest's place or in a basket to be picked up as everyone leaves. Or if you aren't the pickling type, cornichons (tiny baby pickles) are perfect. Or have a packet of watermelon seeds for each guest to take home. You can include strict instructions "these seeds are not for swallowing."

If you have a scarecrow in your garden, stuff her with a pillow, set her in a watermelon patch, and call her "Any Day Now."

recipes

Bundles of Joy

1 tablespoon butter
1 bunch green onions with tops, chopped
1 teaspoon sugar
1/2 cup balsamic vinegar
1/4 cup brown sugar
1 teaspoon chopped fresh dill
1 clove garlic, minced
4 frozen phyllo sheets, thawed
3 oz. goat cheese
chive tops for garnish

Melt the butter in a large skillet and add the onions and sugar. Cook 7–8 minutes, stirring often. Add the vinegar, brown sugar, dill, and garlic. Cook for 15 more minutes. Stack the phyllo according to the package directions and cut it into 6 5-inch squares. Place the onion mixture onto the center of each square of phyllo, then spread evenly with the goat cheese. Lift the corners of dough and twist them together to form a little bundle. Bake until golden (approximately 10–12 minutes). Before serving, tie a bow with a chive around the top of each bundle.

Yield: 30 bundles

Watermelon Punch with Fresh Fruit Garnish

2 cups water
2/3 cup freshly squeezed lemon or lime juice
2/3 cup sugar
2 cups freshly squeezed orange juice
3 ounces frozen pineapple concentrate
1 large oblong watermelon
Mint leaves for garnish
Crushed ice

Bring the water, lemon or lime juice, and sugar to a boil in a saucepan. Let boil for 3–4 minutes or until the consistency is syrupy. Cool completely and stir in the orange juice and pineapple concentrate. Scoop out two cups of watermelon using a melon ball cutter and refrigerate them. Scoop out the remaining watermelon, discarding seeds, and process it in blender until it's smooth. Pour through a wire mesh strainer reserving 3 cups of juice. Discard any pulp. Mix the watermelon juice with the juice mixture and chill. When ready to serve, pour the punch into the watermelon baby carriage punch bowl. Float the reserved melon balls in the punch. Fill glasses with crushed ice and garnish with mint leaves and let your guests serve themselves.

Blue Cheese Tater Tots
(Blue Cheese New Potatoes)

2 pounds small new potatoes, quartered
1 tablespoon butter
1 cup green onion, chopped
3/4 cup whipping cream
1 tablespoon all-purpose flour
2 ounces crumbled blue cheese
Salt and pepper to taste
2 tablespoons chopped fresh parsley
4 slices bacon, cooked crisp

Cook the potatoes in water to cover until they're tender (approximately 15 minutes) and drain. Toss the potatoes with the butter and onion in a bowl. Over medium heat, mix together the whipping cream and flour in a saucepan. Stir constantly for 3 minutes, adding the blue cheese as you stir. Fold the salt and pepper into the potato mixture. Just before serving, top with parsley and bacon.

Yield: 8 to 10 servings

Due-Date Nut Bars

1/2 cup butter
1/2 cup brown sugar
1 egg
6 tablespoons whole milk
1 cup chopped dates
1 cup chopped pecans
1/2 cup grated carrot
1/4 cup all-purpose flour
1/2 teaspoon baking powder
1/4 teaspoon salt
1 teaspoon cinnamon
2/3 cup old-fashioned oats
Juice of 1 lime

Preheat oven to 325 degrees. Cream together the butter and sugar. Add the egg, milk, dates, pecans, and carrots, and beat well. Sift together the flour, baking powder, salt, and cinnamon, and add the oats, mixing well. Combine the wet and dry ingredients and add lime juice. Spread the mixture onto a greased and floured 7$\frac{1}{2}$ by 11$\frac{3}{4}$ pan and bake for 20 minutes.

Yield: 24 bars

Baby Picture, Shelley Snow, watercolor

Veggie Triplets (Broccoli Florets with Carrot and Zucchini Squash Ribbons)

3 large carrots
3 medium zucchini
2 cups broccoli florets
1 cup prepared basil pesto or sun-dried tomato pesto
2 tablespoons balsamic vinegar
1 teaspoon sugar

Using a vegetable peeler, cut ribbon-like slices from the carrots and zucchini. In a saucepan, bring 2 inches of water to a boil. Add all the vegetables and cook 2–3 minutes, covered. Drain well. Meanwhile, combine the pesto, vinegar, and sugar and toss with warm vegetables.

Yield: 6 to 8 servings

Cherry Tomato Salad with Spanked Baby Bottom Dressing on Bibb Lettuce

For each individual salad:

1 head Bibb lettuce, cored
Cherry tomatoes, halved
5–6 Kirby cucumber slices
6–7 capers, drained
3 rings purple onion, thinly sliced
5–6 jumbo pitted black olives

Arrange the lettuce on salad plate. Place tomatoes, cucumbers, capers, and onion on the lettuce-lined plate. Spoon the dressing over all and top with the black olives.

Spanked Baby Bottom Dressing:

1 cup real mayonnaise
1 tablespoon ketchup
2 tablespoons cider vinegar
Salt and pepper to taste

Combine all ingredients until smooth and creamy.

Seed Packets, Elaine Husband, watercolor

Peachy Pink Ice Cream

(Serve ice cream with kosher dill midgets, baby dill gherkins, and jumbo olives)

- 1 (14-ounce) can sweetened condensed milk
- 1 (12-ounce) can evaporated milk
- 2 cups whole milk
- 3 eggs
- 1 cup sugar
- 3 cups whipping cream
- 1 pint fresh or frozen strawberries, chopped
- 3 medium peaches, peeled and finely chopped
- Fresh fruit slices and fresh mint leaves for garnish

Whisk together the milks, eggs, and sugar in a saucepan and cook over medium heat, stirring constantly, for approximately 10 minutes. Remove from the heat and let cool. Beat the whipping cream until soft peaks form. Stir the whipped cream and chopped fruit into milk mixture. Pour into an ice-cream freezer container and freeze according to the manufacturer's instructions. Garnish with fresh fruit slices and fresh mint leaves.

Any Day Now, Shelley Snow, watercolor

The Garden Ladies

In the spring of 1994, we planted a garden together. It was now the hottest day in July, and we were having lunch, enjoying the fruits of our labor—a fabulous tomato sandwich, piled high with cucumber slices, fresh basil, and mayonnaise. Ice clinked in our tall glasses of cold mint tea as we gestured toward the weeds left yet to pull, or not to pull, in the insufferable 98-degree heat. Even our garden lady, our feminine scarecrow, was wilting under the pressure.

We decided to give her a new outfit. Another old garden hat and apron? No. We decided she deserved a real makeover. We weren't really sure what look we wanted to give her, or what outfits we were willing to part with, so we discarded her faded, mildewed garb and draped her in an old bathrobe until we determined her new look. Well, she might as well have some bunny slippers . . . and curlers . . . and a hair net to hold the curlers on her head that had no hair. Slippers we had, but the curlers and the hair net would require a quick trip to the dollar store.

This was fun! By the next morning, we had a grand plan. We had gone through our closets, drawers, and attics and pulled out every conceivable article of clothing and accessories that would give her not one new look, but a whole wardrobe of chic new outfits for any occasion. Had we lost our minds? We were playing dress-up with a couple of sticks and a stuffed head. But we were having so much fun, and that hot day in July, the needle on the laughter meter went off the scale.

When we started going through our stuff and realized all the different options we could give our garden lady, we couldn't decide on one particular attire. But when we looked at her in her robe and curlers, we realized we loved the way she looked and the personality she had become. So we named her Morning Glory, and we decided we would just build another one. What could be wrong with two garden ladies?

The next one that emerged from our pile of choices was an artist. We had plenty of old paint smocks and all the gear to make her authentic enough to be called Fran Go. She was so cute, she had to stay. What was the harm in having three garden ladies? Well, the next thing we knew, we had garden ladies all over the garden and the yard.

There was Marrygold, the bride, in her lace tablecloth with her wedding veil and satin shoes that had belonged to one of our daughters. There was Miss Vidalia, the tea lady, dressed to the nines in her garden party hat, white gloves, and faux pearls. Low-Fat Pat, the weight watcher, was so cool in her slenderizing getup, and Whatta Tomato was the real dish of the garden. Try to picture this. By the end of that day, there were at least a dozen stick ladies in different outfits, representing different careers and with definite personalities, drawing quite a bit of attention from bewildered neighbors and passersby.

But the one we really had the most fun with was the one that made us practically pass out from laughing. Have you ever tried to tie a pillow to a stick, put a dress on it, and stand it up straight in a watermelon patch? Well, we did, and, for obvious reasons, we named her "Any Day Now."

CHAPTER NINE
A Little Twilight Magic
A Dinner Party Honoring the Bride and Groom

For this blessed event, we have chosen an intimate and memorable garden dinner. The occasion is beautiful from the first bird's song through lingering moonlight. We chose twilight for its unique ability to create an atmosphere of pale gold light and long blue shadows. The following ideas are some of our own we have used to decorate bridal parties for our friends and family. Whether the setting is as simple as a meadow with a single flute playing, or as elaborate as a formal garden with a symphony, these ideas will make it truly unforgettable.

Menu Suggestions

*Cold Vegetable Tart
*Pickled Shrimp with Cherry Tomatoes and Olives
*Fresh Fruit Bowl with Honey Lime Yogurt
*Shiitake Mushroom, Baby Beet, and Yellow Pepper Salad
*Risotto with Prosciutto
*Fruit-Glazed Custard Tarts

Twilight Magic, Elaine Husband, acrylic

We suggest serving beef tenderloin and hot, buttered French bread with this menu.

Twilight Magic Special Effects

Whether you're blessed with an expansive lawn surrounded by luscious antique roses and formal gardens or a simple backyard patio, you can transform any setting into a magical twilight affair.

Mix fruits and vegetables with your flowers to create these stunning arrangements:

Green hydrangea blossoms, green grape clusters, and limes, combined with Queen Anne's lace, white peonies or roses

Lilac blossoms, peaches and lemons, lavender and peach roses

Hot pink, red, and orange zinnias; red poppies; bright yellow sunflowers; deep blue delphinium; black-eyed Susans combined with bright yellow, red, and orange peppers; dark purple plums and artichokes

Pink tulips and roses, bells of Ireland, pink stock and peonies, combined with fresh asparagus, artichokes, and green grape clusters

Blue hydrangea blossoms, black grapes, and shiny green apples

White market umbrellas make romantic wedding canopies above each table. Here, a white theme is especially beautiful. Measure the circumference of the edge of the umbrella, add two yards, and cut that measurement from white tulle. Loosely scallop the tulle around the umbrella's edge, gathering and securing it at each spoke with white satin ribbon. Using a small bouquet holder containing an oasis, make small bouquets of white flowers. Allow some greenery and flowers to spill down gracefully.

Arrange the floral centerpieces at the center of the tables and the base of the umbrella poles. A circular gelatin mold filled with a soaked oasis makes an ideal container for your arrangement. If you don't have molds, use two containers on either side of the pole. Fill them with the flowers of your choice and mix with rich green ivy or airy asparagus fern.

Lovely Victorian birdcages make beautiful and unique additions to the party site. Place bouquets of fresh flowers with cascading ribbons on each birdcage and attach them with wire. Be creative and make every bouquet a different shape and size. Bridesmaid bouquet holders with floral oasis blocks work perfectly for this. Hang them from tree branches or birdcage stands, or place them on stone pedestals, garden steps, on either side of your front door, or any spot you want a beautiful touch.

Old picnic baskets, gathered from friends and garage sales, are other old-fashioned containers for fresh flowers. Placed on old quilts around the yard with lacy linens tucked around them, they give a "homey" welcome to your guests. One distinctive basket of flowers makes a perfect centerpiece for your food table.

Paint old chandeliers, found at junk stores or garage sales, white and hang them from tree branches. Small clay pots, painted white to match the fixtures, can be glued where each light was. Fill the pot with a floral oasis block, place a candle in the middle, and surround with hanging greenery and flowers. What could be more romantic than candlelight in the trees?

A mossy-covered stone cherub, a garden angel, or other stone statuary is lovely as the focal point of your food table or your garden.

If you have a scarecrow, dress her like a bride and call her "Marrygold."

recipes

Cold Vegetable Tart

- 1 (5-ounce) package vegetable crackers
- 1/3 cup real mayonnaise
- 2 (8-ounce) packages cream cheese, softened
- 1/2 cup finely chopped broccoli florets
- 1/2 cup finely chopped red bell pepper
- 1/3 cup finely chopped green onions with tops
- 1/3 cup grated Parmesan cheese
- 2 teaspoons ranch-style salad dressing mix
- 1/4 teaspoon garlic powder
- 1 teaspoon Worcestershire sauce
- 1 French baguette, sliced, buttered, and baked until crisp

Process the crackers until they resemble fine crumbs. Combine them with the mayonnaise and press the mixture into bottom of a 9-inch springform pan. Beat the cream cheese until smooth and add the broccoli, bell pepper, green onions, Parmesan cheese, salad dressing mix, garlic powder, and Worcestershire sauce. Mix well. Spread the mixture over the crust; cover it and chill overnight. To serve, remove the sides from pan and place the tart on a platter. Guests can spread on crisp baguette rounds.

Yield: About 24 servings

Marrygold, Elaine Husband, watercolor

Pickled Shrimp with Cherry Tomatoes and Olives

4 cups water
1 package crab boil
1½ pounds unpeeled medium fresh shrimp, unpeeled
1 (16-ounce) bottle Italian dressing (not fat-free)
3–4 drops hot sauce
1 cup cherry tomatoes
1 (14-ounce) can artichoke hearts, drained and quartered
1 cup Greek black olives
2 cups button mushrooms
Lettuce

Bring the water, crab boil, and shrimp to a boil and cook 3–5 minutes. Drain well and rinse in cold water. Peel and devein the shrimp and combine them with ½ bottle of Italian dressing and the hot sauce in a heavy-duty locking plastic bag. Refrigerate for 24 hours, turning the bag occasionally. Repeat this process for the cherry tomatoes, artichoke hearts, olives, and mushrooms, using the remaining half of the dressing. Drain the shrimp and vegetables and serve them in a lettuce-lined bowl.

Yield: About 24 servings

Fresh Fruit Bowl with Honey Lime Yogurt

3 cups fresh whole strawberries (do not hull)
3 cups sliced fresh peaches
1 cup fresh blueberries
1 cup fresh blackberries
1 bunch fresh mint for garnish

Grapes and Wine, Shelley Snow, watercolor

Honey Lime Dressing

¼ cup frozen orange juice concentrate
2 tablespoons honey
4 teaspoons fresh lime juice
1 cup plain yogurt
2 cups honeydew melon cubes

Put the strawberries, peaches, and blueberries in large serving bowl. (Reserve blackberries until last minute.) Combine the dressing ingredients in a blender and process until smooth. Just before serving, add the blackberries, pour the dressing over all, and garnish with mint leaves.

Yield: About 16 servings

Roses, Shelley Snow, watercolor

Shiitake Mushroom, Baby Beet, and Yellow Pepper Salad

¾ cup red wine vinegar
½ cup olive oil
1 garlic clove, minced
½ teaspoon salt
¼ teaspoon freshly ground pepper
2 teaspoons Dijon mustard
2 (3½-ounce) packages shiitake
   mushrooms, sliced, washed,
   and stems cut off
1 cup whole baby beets, drained
2 large yellow bell peppers, sliced in rings
10 cups mixed fresh salad greens
1 (4-ounce) package crumbled feta cheese

Combine the vinegar, olive oil, garlic, salt, pepper, and Dijon mustard in a large jar and shake vigorously. Pour over the mushrooms, beets, and yellow pepper in a large bowl; cover and chill overnight. To serve, arrange the drained beets, mushrooms, and peppers over greens on each salad plate. Sprinkle with the feta cheese and drizzle with the vinegar mixture.

Yield: About 10 servings

Risotto with Prosciutto

2 cups arborio rice
4 cups chicken broth
1/3 cup diced red bell pepper
2 medium leeks (white part only),
   finely chopped
1/2 cup fresh shelled green peas
2 tablespoons plus 2 tablespoons butter
1/3 cup diced mild green chilies
2 1/2 ounces prosciutto (coarsely chopped)
1 cup sour cream
1 cup shredded Monterey Jack cheese
1 cup freshly grated Parmesan cheese
Salt and pepper to taste (optional)

Dream Cycle, Elaine Husband, acrylic

Preheat oven to 450 degrees. Cook the rice in the chicken broth until tender. Saute the bell peppers, leeks, and peas in 2 tablespoons of butter until tender. Combine with the green chilies and add to the rice mixture. Add the proscuitto to the rice mixture and place in an 11-by-8 inch baking dish. Add salt and pepper if desired. Combine the sour cream and Monterey Jack and spread evenly over the rice. Sprinkle the top with Parmesan cheese and dot with the remaining butter. Bake 15 minutes or until top is golden and puffy.

Yield: 10 servings

Fruit-Glazed Custard Tarts

3 eggs
1/2 cup sugar
1/4 teaspoon salt
2 cups light cream
1 teaspoon almond or vanilla extract
12 (3-inch) prebaked tart shells
1 cup red currant jelly
1 tablespoon rum

Fruit for garnish: pitted dark cherries, blueberries, kiwi slices, peach slices, raspberries, thin twists of lemon or lime, mint leaves. Preheat oven to 325 degrees. Beat the eggs slightly, add the sugar, salt, light cream, and extract; stir well. Pour into tart shells and bake for approximately 30 minutes. Cool the tarts, then add fruit garnish. Top each tart with a different fruit. Melt the jelly over low heat, add a tablespoon of rum, and allow to cool slightly, then coat the fruit with the glaze. Serve on a tiered dessert stand.

That Sinking Feeling

It was 1964, and we were seniors in high school. We had been cheerleaders since seventh grade, and by now we were pretty sick of it. Don't get us wrong; we were full of school spirit and loved our team, but this was tournament time, our team never lost, and we had never missed a game. This was the final regional basketball tournament in the freezing cold of February.

On this particular night, we were exhausted from cheering the last four nights, getting to bed late and having to get up early. Since one of our homes was on the way to the game, the pep bus was going to stop and pick us up. We said that if "the Blue Goose" (the 1950 faded denim blue Plymouth) wasn't parked in the driveway, it meant we had driven ourselves to the game. At least, that was the plan. However, the plan "fell through."

As we sat in the car waiting for the bus, the thought of going to one more game became more than we could endure. So we concocted a new plan. If the bus driver didn't see the car, he would proceed to the game without us. Therefore, we'd just move the car. In fact, we could just drive it around the house and hide it in the backyard! Then we could go back in the warm house, fix peanut butter and mayonnaise sandwiches topped with a couple of sour pickles, and watch TV. Our parents were out for the night, so we didn't see any obstacles to this perfect plan.

There was one hidden obstacle, however. As we drove around the side of the house into the backyard, feeling so pleased with ourselves and our ingenious plan, the car suddenly wouldn't go another inch. Not worried, we gunned the gas pedal thinking we were stuck just a little—but the car didn't move. Well, that's not completely accurate. It did move—down. Talk about that sinking feeling! It happened so fast we didn't think to simply open the door and get out. By the time we finally did, the door wasn't an option. Finally, when the initial shock wore off, we escaped through the only window in the old wreck that would ever roll down.

Once we got out of the car, the mystery was solved and became crystal clear. Well, maybe not so crystal—more like murky. We had driven right smack over the septic tank and were ankle-deep in all of its trappings. The "Blue Goose" had landed, and so had we, for the next two weeks anyway.

CHAPTER TEN
An Angel Luncheon
A Heavenly Luncheon for the Special Angels in Your Life

Angels are ministering spirits. There are times when you may want to honor the people who have been ministering spirits in your life. Whether they've gone out of their way to help you, or have been a constant source of encouragement, or have endeared themselves to you in some inexplicable way, they have truly blessed you and made your life richer. It could be a teacher, a neighbor, a close friend's mother, or even a grocery checker who stands on her feet all day but never fails to give you her brightest smile. This is a luncheon to honor those people and let them know their kindness has not gone unnoticed or unappreciated.

Nothing could be lovelier or more appropriate than having this luncheon in a garden. Whether you make it a picnic from a basket, or a seated affair with your finest china, this occasion should become a blessing that neither your guests, nor you, will ever forget.

Stargazer Lilies, Shelley Snow, watercolor

Menu Suggestions (Angel Food):

*Celestial Tea
*Holy Roll-Ups (Stuffed Grape Leaves)
*Heavenly Halos (Asparagus Ring Molds)
Chicken Divine
*A Host of Summer Vegetables over Angel Hair Pasta
Angel Biscuits
*Angel Food Cake with Fresh Fruit and Whipped Cream Clouds
Bible Belts (Liqueur-Flavored Coffee)

Angel Luncheon Special Effects

Include the names of your honored guests on the front of the invitation so that each will know that she is one of the "angels." Send along the menu as well.

At each place setting:

Make or buy an angelic card and place a personal note inside stating the reasons why the guest has earned her wings and is an angel to you.

On each plate place a halo made from gold or silver star garland for each person to wear.

Bake a small batch of angel-shaped cookies, iced in white robes, gold wings, and halos. Wrap in gift-wrap cellophane, tie with a star garland, and place at each setting for the honorees to take home. (Angel cookie cutters are easy to find at kitchen specialty shops.)

"Gardening angels," found at local gift shops or garden centers, make ideal place cards, with a name tag for each guest. Honorees can keep these.

The centerpiece for your table should be ethereal. If you have a stone angel in your garden, it makes a striking centerpiece surrounded by fresh greenery, such as ivy. Place a garland of fresh flowers on the angel's head.

Another centerpiece idea is to use your beautifully decorated angel food cake as your focal point. Ice your cake

Stone Angel, Shelley Snow, watercolor

with whipped cream clouds (see recipe). Place a slim vase in the center hole of the cake and fill it with roses. Surround the cake's base with sugared raspberries. Make sure you put your cake on a 4- or 5-inch cake stand. To elevate

Angel Biscuit, Shelley Snow, watercolor

the cake further, place a round silver tray on top of a silver Revere bowl, then center the cake stand on the tray. Surround the cake stand base with small silver vases (silver baby cups, mint julep cups, etc.) containing more roses.

For a more simple yet just as lovely effect, fill a crystal vase with stargazer lilies.

A divine touch would be to have harp music playing in your garden.

If it's something within your budget, it would be a heavenly gesture to give each angel a gift certificate to a day spa for a manicure, pedicure, massage, or any other pampering luxury that makes them feel as special as they are. Let your guests see the angel watching over your garden by dressing up a scarecrow to look angelic and calling her "Angel Biscuit."

recipes

Celestial Tea

8 cups water
3 family-size tea bags
1½ cups sugar
3 cups chopped fresh mint leaves
1 cup pineapple juice
1 cup fresh lime juice
Fresh mint sprigs for garnish

Bring 4 cups of water to a boil, add the tea bags and let steep for 5 minutes. Remove the tea bags. Bring the remaining 4 cups of water to a boil and add the sugar and mint leaves. Stir and let stand for 20 minutes. Pour the mint mixture through a wire mesh strainer and discard the leaves. Combine the mint mixture and tea and stir in the lime juice and pineapple juice. Garnish with fresh mint sprig, chill, and serve over ice.

Yield: About 12 to 15 servings

Holy Roll-Ups (Stuffed Grape Leaves)

¾ cup long-grain rice, cooked according to package directions
1 tablespoon chopped fresh mint
¼ cup chopped fresh parsley
6 green onions with tops, chopped
⅛ cup olive oil
¾ teaspoon salt
½ teaspoon ground black pepper
1 tablespoon fresh lemon juice
8–10 grape leaves in vinegar brine

Combine all of the ingredients, except the grape leaves, in a bowl and mix well. Wash and dry the grape leaves and remove their stems. Place the leaves on flat, clean surface with the wide end toward you. Place 2 tablespoons of the rice mixture in the center of each leaf. Fold both sides to the middle, then roll the leaf into a small, firm roll. Refrigerate until ready to serve.

Yield: 6 to 8 servings

Heavenly Halos
(**Asparagus Ring Molds**)

1 pound fresh asparagus, trimmed
2 cups water
1 package unflavored gelatin, dissolved in
    ¼ cup cold water
2 tablespoons capers, drained
½ cup real mayonnaise
1 teaspoon dried tarragon
½ cup heavy cream, whipped
½ teaspoon salt
2 tablespoons lemon juice
½ cup slivered almonds
Mayonnaise and curled lemon slices
    for garnish

Dice the asparagus, and cook in the 2 cups of water until tender. Drain and reserve 1 cup of the hot liquid. Plunge the asparagus into cold water to stop the cooking process and drain well. Pour the reserved hot liquid over the gelatin mixture to dissolve it, then chill until partially set. Mix the capers and tarragon into the mayonnaise and whipped cream, and fold into gelatin. Add the asparagus, salt, lemon juice, and slivered almonds. Pour into individual oiled ring molds and refrigerate until firm. Garnish with a dollop of mayonnaise and a curled lemon slice in center of mold.

Yield: 8 to 10 molds

Asparagus, Elaine Husband, watercolor

A Host of Summer Vegetables over Angel Hair Pasta

6–8 homegrown tomatoes, chopped
1 cup chopped and loosely packed fresh basil
1 red bell pepper, chopped
1 yellow bell pepper, chopped
1 green bell pepper, chopped
1 medium onion, chopped
1 cup eggplant, peeled and chopped
2 cloves garlic, crushed
1/4 cup chopped fresh dill
1/4 cup fresh chives, chopped
4 tablespoons olive oil
1/4 cup balsamic vinegar
Salt and pepper to taste
1 (16-ounce) package angel hair pasta
1 cup whole black olives
1/2 cup freshly grated Parmesan cheese

Put tomatoes and their juice in a bowl with the fresh basil and set aside for 4–5 hours. When you're ready to prepare the dish, sauté the peppers, onions, eggplant, garlic, dill, and chives in the olive oil just until tender. Do not overcook them. Drain the excess oil from pan and add the vinegar, salt, and pepper. Meanwhile, boil the pasta according to package directions and drain. Just before serving, add the tomatoes and basil to the vegetable mixture, and heat just until the tomatoes are warm, but not cooked. Fold in the olives. Spoon the sauce over the cooked pasta, sprinkle with fresh Parmesan cheese, and serve.

Yield: 12 servings

Angel Food Cake with Fresh Fruit and Whipped Cream Clouds

1 cup cake flour
1/2 cup plus 1 cup sugar
1 1/2 cups egg whites (10–12 eggs), room temperature
2 1/2 tablespoons cold water
1 1/2 teaspoons cream of tartar
1/4 teaspoon vanilla
1 teaspoon almond extract
1/2 teaspoon salt

Preheat oven to 350 degrees. Sift the flour and 1/2 cup of sugar at least six times. Combine the egg whites, cold water, cream of tartar, vanilla, almond extract, and salt in a mixing bowl and beat until stiff, but not dry. The mixture should be glossy. Fold in the remaining cup of sugar, 2 tablespoons at a time. Pour into an ungreased tube pan and bake for 45 minutes. To cool, invert the pan and let the cake remain inside for 1 1/2 hours.

Fresh Fruit and Whipped Cream Clouds

1/2 cup seedless raspberry jam
2 cups whipping cream, whipped
1/2 cup sifted confectioner's sugar
1/4 cup sour cream
3 cups fresh raspberries
1/2 cup sugar (for frosting berries)

Melt the jam over low heat and set aside. Cut the angel food cake in half, crosswise. Beat the whipping cream until foamy and gradually add the confectioner's sugar until soft peaks form. Add the sour cream and beat until stiff peaks form. Spread the jam over the bottom half of cake. Top with a layer of raspberries, then whipped cream, then cover with the top half of cake. Frost the cake generously with the whipped cream. Roll the raspberries in sugar and arrange them on top and around the base of the cake.

Coconut Cake, Shelley Snow, watercolor

Hong-e-Long-Long

We were about ten years old, give or take a year. It was a summer night, and we were camping out in the backyard under our clothesline "tent." We had just finished our delectable supper of peanut butter and mayonnaise sandwiches, a jar of dill pickles, and red Kool-Aid. We decided this was the perfect night to make up a secret language because we were sick and tired of our sisters and brothers understanding what we were talking about. And we wanted to say "hell!"

Curse words were forbidden, of course, so we decided that if we could invent a completely different language, we could use curse words and be totally undetected (as if our parents couldn't decode).

We can't remember exactly how we devised the mechanics of this cool lingo, but here's the way it worked. Every word is spelled letter by letter, using "ong" after every consonant but saying the vowels. For example: the word, "hell," is pronounced "hong-e-long-long." To this day, hong-e-long-long is our favorite word, not because it says "hell" but because it conjures up such an innocent and carefree time in our lives.

We soon found out our secret language wasn't such a secret. We came home from school one day after a fateful call from a teacher, and found a message from our mothers that read: "Yong-o-u a-rong-e gong-rong-o-u-nong-dong-e-dong!" (You are grounded!)

CHAPTER ELEVEN
Fit to Eat
Low Fat, High Fun

Since everyone is watching her weight these days, this low-fat luncheon features attractive and delicious recipes that cater to the spandex-wearing "wanna-bes." Here is a yummy, guilt-free menu that's more than "fit to eat." This get-together is perfect for your exercise group, your walking buddies, your tennis partners, or any friends who are fighting the "battle of the bulge."

Your invitations can suggest taking a break from the seriousness of the whole thing, and poking a little fun at yourselves.

Menu Suggestions

*Garlic Eggplant Spread on Toasted Baguette Slices

Salmon Filets

*Fresh Vegetable Salsa

Pineapple Salsa

*"Fit to Eat" Mashed Potatoes

Mixed Green Salad

*Banana Split Buffet

Still Life with Blue Goblet, Shelley Snow, watercolor

Fit to Eat Special Effects

Let's make this a guilt-free gathering by plopping your bathroom scales in the middle of the lunch table so even the most obsessive dieter can't weigh herself! It'll be fun and it makes a great base for a centerpiece of fresh flowers or candles, etc.

For place cards, here's a new way to use green onions, carrots, and celery . . . create skinny little women out of the natural shapes of these vegetables. For example, a green onion makes an adorable lady with the onion bulb as her head, the roots as her hair, and the green tops spread out as her skirt. Toothpicks are her oh-so-slender arms. Attach her to a base by tying a thin ribbon around her tiny waist so she can stand. Carrots, broccoli, and celery may not have such a shapely figure, but they're just as cute with their big hair.

To remember this gathering for a long time, take each guest's picture. As a prop, paint a foxy, curvy, lightweight lady on a large piece of cardboard or heavy paper, leaving a hole where the face should be. Each friend sticks her own face through the opening and has her picture taken looking like a swimsuit model.

Have each friend bring an inexpensive door prize relating to anything about health and fitness. A low-fat cookbook, a calorie counter, or one of those workout tapes you never use would be ideal.

To greet your low-fat friends, make a door decoration of two bunches of fresh carrots with their feathery tops and tie them securely with a bow made from a cloth measuring tape.

recipes

Garlic Eggplant Spread on Toasted Baguette Slices

Vegetable cooking spray
2 large eggplants, peeled and cut into thin slices
1/4 cup chopped fresh basil
2 green onions with tops, chopped
1/2 teaspoon coarsely ground black pepper
1 tablespoon chopped flat Italian parsley
1/2 cup commercial red wine vinaigrette
1 garlic clove, minced
1 baguette
1/4 cup feta cheese, crumbled
3–4 small homegrown tomatoes, sliced 1/4-inch thick
1/2 teaspoon salt

Preheat oven to 350 degrees. Coat a baking sheet with cooking spray. Place the eggplant slices on the pan and bake until tender, about 20 minutes. Remove from the pan and place in an airtight container with the basil, onion tops, salt, pepper, parsley, vinaigrette, and garlic. Chill overnight. Preheat the broiler. Drain the liquid from the eggplant mixture and place it in a food processor and process until smooth. Cut the bread into 1/2-inch slices, and toast it lightly. Spread some eggplant mixture on each toast. Top each one with 1 tomato slice, sprinkle it with cheese, and place under a broiler for about 3 minutes, or just until the cheese melts.

Yield: Approximately 12 servings

Scale with Flowers, Elaine Husband, watercolor

Fresh Vegetable Salsa

8 ears fresh corn
2 medium tomatoes, chopped
½ green bell pepper, chopped
½ red bell pepper, chopped
½ medium sweet onion, chopped
2–3 small (Kirby) cucumbers, peeled and chopped
½ cup light sour cream
¼ cup low-fat mayonnaise
2 tablespoons red wine vinegar
1 tablespoon Worcestershire sauce
1 teaspoon sugar
1 tablespoon chopped parsley
Salt and freshly ground pepper
1 medium avocado

Remove and discard the husks and silk from the corn and cook the ears for 5 minutes in boiling water. Drain and cut the kernels from cob. Combine the tomatoes, peppers, onion, cucumbers, and corn in a large bowl. Mix the sour cream, mayonnaise, red wine vinegar, Worcestershire sauce, sugar, parsley, and salt and pepper in a separate bowl and pour it over vegetables. Marinate in refrigerator for at least 3 hours. Just before serving, chop and add the avocado to the salsa mixture. Serve as an accompaniment to salmon.

Veggie Ladies, Elaine Husband, acrylic

"Fit to Eat" Mashed Potatoes

3 1/2 pounds new potatoes, quartered
1 can nonfat chicken broth
3 stalks celery, halved across the width
1 medium onion, chopped
3/4 cup buttermilk
8 ounces reduced-fat loaf process
 cheese spread, cubed
Freshly ground pepper

Cook potatoes in enough water to cover, then add the chicken broth, celery, and onion. Simmer until potatoes are tender. Drain and discard the celery. On very low heat, mash the potatoes, stirring in the buttermilk, cheese cubes, and pepper. Stir just until cheese melts, being careful not to let the cheese burn. To serve, put the potatoes in a low-temperature oven until they are heated thoroughly (about 10 minutes).

Yield: 8 to 10 servings

Mixed Green Salad

Fresh spring greens tossed with your favorite low-fat salad dressing

Banana Split Buffet

1 banana per serving
Frozen low-fat vanilla yogurt or ice cream
Low-fat whipped topping
Chocolate, butterscotch, caramel
 ice cream syrups
Chopped almonds, walnuts, pecans
Strawberries, raspberries, blueberries,
 peaches, cherries, pineapple

For each dessert, slice a banana in half along its length. Place in individual serving dishes, topped with 2 or 3 scoops of ice cream or yogurt. Serve the toppings buffet style, and let each guest create his or her own scrumptious finale.

Working the Neighborhood

The scene of some of our more elaborate plots and projects centered around our neighborhood, so, it was not uncommon for some of our neighbors to keep their doors locked and their blinds closed at all times. It wasn't so much that we would do them any harm; they were more afraid of the harm they might do us. Many times the response to our knock on their door was a little voice, coming from out of nowhere, saying, "We are not home." All we wanted to do was to ask them a couple of dozen questions, charge them to see our traveling magic show, or, for a small fee, give them a chance to see our live exotic zoo, which consisted of a baby alligator named Lassie and Cleopatra, the nanny goat that did handstands.

Well, maybe we had tried their patience a little. Maybe dressing up in our Dragnet outfits, knocking on neighbors' doors asking for "Just the facts, Ma'am, just the facts," had gotten a little old. Maybe we had overworked the side of the road scene, with the ketchup blood on one of us and the other flagging down cars for help. And, yes, maybe we had faked too many ghost appearances. So, maybe it was time we tried a new angle.

Even as young children, we loved to make up recipes. Why not capitalize on this passion? We perfected one recipe that we thought might be a big seller and, in fact, had tried to offer it to a few of our friends. They passed it up, but maybe our neighbors would test it for us, and like it so much they would place regular orders for it.

Since we lacked financial backing, our ingredients had to be whatever we could find around the house. Leftovers might be considered as filler, but we had our own definite likes and dislikes, which determined how the end product would taste and look. If we put everything we loved to eat in one giant pot, how could it not be delicious?

Fired up, we set out to put first things first. We found a bunch of old jars with tops in the basement and washed them thoroughly with the hose. Then we made labels on which we drew pictures of the food inside, painted them, glued them to the jars, and priced them according to size. A baby food-sized jar was ten cents, a quart-sized mayonnaise jar, fifty cents, and a gallon-sized pickle jar, a dollar.

Our marketing strategy was to draw and post signs all over the neighborhood that read: "GRAND OPENING! We have invented a new food. Please come and try it. It's cheap and very delicious. It goes with everything because it has everything in it. ELAINE AND SHELLEY'S DRIVE-IN. Drive in the driveway and we will bring it to your car. Delivery can be arranged."

After we made the signs, we collected all available ingredients from out mother's pantries and refrigerators. Obviously, our mothers weren't home at the time. When we finally got everything into the pot, we turned it on to cook. We thought it needed to be on high because it was so big, and we wanted it to hurry and be ready in time for the first customers. We figured as soon as we got the signs up, people would start "driving in."

While the pot was cooking, we decided it was time to advertise. We set off with our signs, completely canvassing the neighborhood, using every telephone pole and fence post. By the time we returned home, we realized our new business venture had gone up in smoke, literally. All we could think of was how disappointed our neighbors would be to find out that our "Drive-In" would never open, we would never be rich, and we would never get to wear those paper hats that all the carhops at the "drive-in" got to wear.

CHAPTER TWELVE
Top of the Hill Birthday
Celebrating the Best That Is Yet to Be

When you turn forty, you may wake up to a sign in your front yard proclaiming to the world, "Lordy, Lordy, you just turned forty!" However, we believe it's really "nifty to turn fifty!"

This fiftieth birthday gathering is a new and unique approach to reaching middle age that emphasizes the best is yet to be. The reward of reaping the harvest comes after long hours of sowing and tilling. And comparable to a garden, a person's life reflects the same truth. Celebrate! You are at the "top of the hill," not "over the hill." From this panoramic view, you can see all the valleys and the paths you chose to get to where you stand now. The best part of it all is that now you see the sky and all the distant horizons that beckon you. The journey to this pinnacle has given you the wisdom and the courage to determine which new horizons to seek and which roads to leave untraveled.

Oftentimes women over fifty are more productive than at any other time in their lives. We write more books, start more businesses, travel more places, and actually do what it takes to make our own lives more fulfilling. Instead of doing what has always been expected of us, we can follow our hearts.

Fiftieth Birthday Cake, Elaine Husband, watercolor

This is not an occasion where your friends make gifts of dentures, 2-inch thick bifocals, hemorrhoid cream, or tombstones with your name carved on them. Rather, this is a day to fly kites, wear purple, eat cake, drink champagne, and share your dreams.

Menu Suggestions

Champagne

Box lunches containing:

*Veggie Wraps
*Homemade Pimento Cheese
*Crunchy Pickles
Fresh Fruit

Dream Cake

Homemade Ice Cream

Top of the Hill Birthday Special Effects

Pick a day, preferably in the spring, summer, or fall, to celebrate your birthday as well as the birthdays of all your friends. When you send your invitations, be sure they understand the celebration is for everyone, not just you. Most important, make sure they know it's a "Top of the Hill," not an "Over the Hill," birthday.

Let them know that this is a "come as you are, drop-in affair."

Instead of gifts for everyone, have an earring swap. Ask people to bring old pairs of earrings they've gotten tired of. Display them attractively and let everyone choose "new" ones. Or:

Let each guest bring a small wrapped gift. When each one arrives, number the gifts and later let each birthday girl draw a number that corresponds to that gift.

Kites, Elaine Husband, acrylic

Make it a garden gift party where all the guests bring something from their own garden that can be transplanted in another garden. One person may have an abundance of a certain variety that would bless someone else's garden. A few good suggestions are bulbs that need to be divided, herbs, onion sets, or tomato plants.

Do something you haven't done in a long time, or thought you were too old to do, for example, give everyone a kite to fly. Not only is a kite symbolic of freedom and flight, it's just a whole lot of plain fun flying one.

Hats, Elaine Husband, acrylic

Go to a discount store and purchase inexpensive straw hats for each person. Buy or collect ribbon, artificial flowers, birds, butterflies, and anything else that speaks to you, to decorate the hats. Everyone can decorate her own hat her own way.

Why not take your shoes off and take a walk in the creek or in the rain? Roll down a hill? Make a clover chain? Blow bubbles?

Stage a "Miss America" pageant. Wear old evening dresses, have a talent competition, ask each other thought-provoking questions, and leave out the swimsuit competition.

Have a scavenger hunt, take a hot-air balloon ride, or stage a Broadway show.

Write an upbeat, positive, fun prediction for each guest and place it in her box lunch.

If you have a scarecrow in your garden, dress her up in her birthday suit and call her "Minnie Pause."

recipes

Box Lunches
Veggie Wraps

Spread Herbed Cream Cheese on a 10-inch flour tortilla

Herbed Cream Cheese

1 (3-ounce) package cream cheese
1 tablespoon real mayonnaise
1/2 teaspoon each minced fresh dill, chives, and basil
Italian dressing (on the side)

With the Herbed Cream Cheese, use any of these combinations:

Roasted red peppers, grated carrots, red leaf lettuce, onion, chopped tomatoes
Avocado, sprouts, sautéed spinach and mushrooms, chopped tomatoes
Chopped artichoke hearts, spinach leaves, sliced black olives, chopped tomatoes

Add slices of your favorite cheese, then roll up the tortilla, secure it with a toothpick, and refrigerate. To serve, slice the tortilla in half, wrap it in parchment paper, and serve it with Italian dressing on the side.

Minnie Pause, Elaine Husband, watercolor

Spread Guacamole on a 10-inch flour tortilla

Guacamole

1 small ripe avocado, such as Haas
Juice of 1/2 lime
1 tablespoon mayonnaise
1 teaspoon finely minced onion
1 teaspoon Worcestershire sauce
Hot sauce to taste
Italian dressing (on the side)

With the Guacamole, use any of these combinations:

Chopped tomatoes, cucumbers, green chilies, black olives
White corn, black beans, cilantro, red peppers, roasted garlic
Refried beans, salsa, cucumbers, lettuce, black olives

Add your favorite cheese, if desired, then roll up the tortilla, secure it with a toothpick, and refrigerate. To serve, slice the tortilla in half, wrap it in parchment paper, and serve it with Italian dressing on the side.

Spread Lemon Mayonnaise on a 10-inch flour tortilla

Lemon Mayonnaise

1/2 cup real mayonnaise
1/4 cup cream cheese
2 tablespoons lemon juice
1 tablespoon chives, chopped
French dressing (on the side)

With the Lemon Mayonnaise, use any of these combinations:

Broccoli, golden raisins, drained pineapple tidbits, grated carrots, chopped cashews
Assorted olive slices, chopped artichoke hearts, purple onion slices, watercress
Blanched asparagus spears, sliced tomatoes, cucumber slices, grated hard-boiled egg

Add your favorite cheese, if desired, then roll up the tortilla, secure it with a toothpick, and refrigerate.

To serve, slice the tortilla in half, wrap it in parchment paper, and serve it with French dressing on the side.

Homemade Pimento Cheese

2 cups grated sharp cheddar cheese (aged white)
2 cups grated Monterey Jack cheese
3/4 cup real mayonnaise
1 (4-ounce) jar diced pimentos, drained
1 (4-ounce) jar sliced black olives
1 tablespoon apple cider vinegar
2 green onions with tops, chopped
1 tablespoon Worcestershire sauce
Hot sauce to taste

In a large mixing bowl, combine all of the ingredients, and refrigerate for up to 8 hours. Place a scoop on a lettuce leaf in a small plastic container with a lid.

Yield: 5 cups

Crunchy Pickles

7 cups thinly sliced cucumbers
2 cups thinly sliced onions
1 1/2 cups apple cider vinegar
1/2 cups sugar
1 teaspoon salt
1 teaspoon mustard seed
1 teaspoon celery seed

Layer the cucumber and onions in a large glass bowl. Combine the vinegar, sugar, salt, mustard seed, and celery seed in a saucepan; bring to a boil and cook for 2 minutes. Remove from the heat and pour the liquid over the cucumbers and onions. When cool, cover and refrigerate for 5 days. This keeps up to 1 month in the refrigerator.

Dream Cake

For your dream cake, order from your bakery a five-layer cake with graduated tiers (similar to a wedding cake). Decorate it yourself with fresh fruit and flowers.

Homemade Ice Cream

For ice cream recipes, refer to Chapter 8: "The Unexpected for the Expecting."

Carnton

Carnton is where we spent much of our childhood and it will forever live in our hearts.

Carnton, an antebellum mansion that has been restored to its original state, is located on the outskirts of our town. Built in 1825, it was a working plantation encompassing thousands of acres of woods, rolling hills, and fertile farmland. As was the case of most plantations in the 1800s, it was self-sufficient, with its kitchen gardens, carriage houses, huge barns, slave quarters, and smokehouse. In addition, it had beautiful formal flower gardens where hoop-skirted ladies entertained their beaus in the late afternoon twilight.

Here in Franklin, Tennessee, one of the bloodiest battles of the Civil War was fought in the immediate area surrounding Carnton Plantation. The mansion itself played a significant role: It was turned into a Confederate hospital during and after the battle. Carnton's owners, the McGavocks, donated a parcel of their land for a Confederate cemetery to bury the soldiers killed there.

By 1950, the plantation was still owned by the McGavock family, but the house was no longer the mansion it once was. When Shelley's family moved here from Texas, Carnton was the only place with enough land to pasture the number of cattle her father had brought with him, so they moved into the big, old house that had been standing empty for several years. And this is where it all began.

We became best friends at the age of four when we met in kindergarten. Practically from that day on, so much of our childhood was centered around

Carnton and the magic-filled days we spent wandering through the woods and creeks, exploring the decaying outbuildings, riding horses on the "north forty," or as far as the boundaries of the property would let us go. Because of the history of the place, we spent hours and hours imagining that we lived back then, pretending we were soldiers, prisoners, or nurses during the war. We dug in the basement for bones, searched the attic for Confederate money, and were always on the lookout for Civil War relics. We were Indian princesses, cowgirls, archaeologists, and explorers.

It was there we were safe in our own world. The house itself held us in its spell with its giant empty upstairs rooms, three-story winding staircase, attic ballroom with its shadowy hiding places, and basement with boundless mysteries just waiting to be solved. We had just as much fun recreating the set of *Elephant Walk* on the huge upstairs veranda as we did listening to rain hit the tin roof while we sat in the attic waiting for ghosts to make an appearance.

The magnificent old trees that surrounded the house created arbors of shade where we spent many a summer afternoon. There was nothing like ice-cold lemonade on those hot days with fresh mint from the springhouse. We loved going to the springhouse. As we walked down the hill to the spring, we could actually feel the cool air from the icy cold spring water rush up to meet us, along with the pungent fragrance of mint, which grew in lush abundance there.

On many hot days, you could usually find us in the creek. Just a wade was never enough. Usually we ended up fully immersed in mud and/or water. It was the perfect Tarzan jungle setting, complete with grapevines.

It was just too enticing not to jump from a grapevine into a couple of feet of soft, squishy mud. Days were spent stacking rocks to dam up a particularly promising swimming hole, or to create a waterfall simply for pure aesthetics. Many an expedition headed up by Lewis and Clark (us) was conducted along the banks of that creek.

The Confederate cemetery was an especially peaceful and beautiful spot, with its huge, gnarled, graceful cedars, and row after row of identical headstones lined up like soldiers on a bed of soft, silky green. We became Molly Pitcher and Dolley Madison dispensing mercy to a battlefield of imaginary and grateful wounded. We tore our pretend petticoats to make pretend bandages for pretend injured heroes.

Today Carnton is a national historic site open to the public. Every day, strangers are guided through its elegant rooms and gardens. For these people, the house has only been a glimpse into a moment of history. During all the years of restoration, the memories of Carnton never lessened for us, and, in fact, we continued to think of it as our own. We still walk the grounds, visit the springhouse, and have been known to wade in the creek and jump in the mud on a hot summer day. Our hearts were full as we watched our children marry under tents spread over the lawn, and our hearts were heavy as we watched the felling of great trees around the house.

Although it is a totally different place now, we feel that whenever we go back there, Carnton comes back to us.

Watermelon, Shelley Snow, watercolor

Index

Note: Italics denote recipes.

A

"Angel Biscuit" (Snow), 110
Angel Food Cake with Fresh Fruit and Whipped Cream Clouds, 115
An Angel Luncheon party, 107-11
"Any Day Now" (Snow), 93
appetizers, *29, 38,* 44, *49,* 69-70, *78, 79, 80-81, 88, 101, 112,* 121, 131-33
Apricot Almond Tart, 81
Art in the Dark party, 63-66
"Asparagus" (Husband), 113

B

"Baby Picture" (Snow), 90
Baked Tomato Casserole, 20
Balmy Black-Eyed Pea Salad, 29
Banana Split Buffet, 123
Banlon sweater incident, 40-41
"barn dirt," 23
Basil Tomato Tart, 19
beef, 14, 98
beverages, *39, 88-89, 112*
Blue Cheese Tater Tots, 89
"Blue Goose," 104-5
"Bread and Cheese" (Snow), 47
"Bringing Indoors Out" (Husband), 24
Bundles of Joy, 88
Buttery Asparagus Roll-Ups, 78

C

Café en Plein Air party, 43-45

Carnton Plantation, 134-36

Celestial Tea, 112

centerpieces for parties, 14-15, 28, 45, 54, 55, 65-66, 76, 86, 98, 99, 109-11, 120

Cezanne's Creamy Fruit Dip for Fruit Palette, 68

"Chatting on the Balcony" (Snow), 81

Cheese Straws, 80-81

Cheesy Tomato Melts, 16

Cherry Tomato Salad with Spanked Baby Bottom Dressing, 91

chicken, 29

chow chow, green tomato, 22-23

Classic Tomato Sandwiches, 20

"Coconut Cake" (Snow), 116

Cold Front Fried Chicken, 29

Cold Vegetable Tart, 100

A Covered Dish Country Supper party, 53-55

Crunchy Pickles, 133

Cucumber Tea Sandwiches, 80

D

Degas's Dilled Cucumber Curls with Smoked Salmon Spread, 69-70

desserts, *31, 39, 48-49, 59, 70, 77, 81, 90, 93, 104, 115, 123*

Dilled Shrimp Canapés, 78

dips, *16, 68, 122, 132*

"doing downtown," 50-51

"Dressed to Chill" Asparagus Pie, 30

Due-Date Nut Bars, 90

E

"Elaine and Shelley's Drive-In," 124-25

F

fairy tea, 82
favors for parties, 36, 55, 66, 76, 77, 87, 109, 111, 120, 129, 130
"Fiftieth Birthday Cake" (Husband), 126
Fit to Eat party, 119-20
"Fit to Eat" Mashed Potatoes, 123
Foggy San Francisco Roll-Ups, 29
"Four O'Clock Tea," 82
Fresh Fruit Bowl with Honey Lime Yogurt Dressing, 101-2
Fresh Vegetable Salsa, 122
Fried Green Tomatoes, 17
Fruit-Glazed Custard Tarts, 104

G

garden parties recollected, 60
"The Garden's Bounty" (Snow), 11
Garlic Eggplant Spread on Toasted Baguette Slices, 121
Gauguin's Great French Macaroons, 70
Green Fruit Salad with Honey Lime Dressing, 38-39
Grilled Vegetables with Tomatoes, 19
Guacamole, 132

H

Ham and Creamy Biscuits, 38
Heavenly Halos, 113
Herbed Cream Cheese, 131
Holy Roll-Ups, 112
Homemade Pimento Cheese, 133
"hong-e-long-long," 117

A Host of Summer Vegetables over Angel Hair Pasta, 114
"Hydrangeas and Pears" (Snow), 5

I

The Indoor-Outdoor Picnic party, 25-28
inventing a new food, 124-25

J

"Japanese Lanterns" (Husband), 2
Le Dome du Fromage Frais, 49
Le Navarin d'Agneau, 46
Lemon Mayonnaise, 132
"Lemonade Stand" (Husband), 61

Les Tartelettes aux Pommes, 49
lighting for picnics, 27, 28, 99
A Little Twilight Magic party, 97-99

M

"May Rain" (Snow), 26
mayonnaise, variations on, *20, 21, 57, 68, 80, 132*
McGavock family (Carnton Plantation), 134
"Miss Vidalia" (Snow), 77
Modigliani's Mount of Olives, 70
Monet's Mayonnaise for Veggie Palette, 68
Morning Glory Orange Slushes, 39

"Morning's Glory" (Husband), 34
"Mr. Hunter's Tomato Stand" (Snow), 16
mummification project, 71-72

O

Oatmeal Cookies, 39

P

Peachy Pink Ice Cream, 93
"Pears" (Snow), 28
Pickled Shrimp with Cherry Tomatoes and Olives, 101
Pissarro's Pepper Artichoke Pizza, 68-69
place cards for parties, 15, 54, 66, 108, 109, 120

Plum Baked Peach Tart, 31
Poires au Vin, 48-49
"Portraits" (Husband), 73

Q

"Queen of the Garden" (Husband), 18
Quiche d'Olives, 48

R

Risotto with Prosciutto, 103
Roasted Corn on the Cob with Cayenne Lime Butter, 56-57
Roasted Pepper and Olive Canapés, 79
"The Rose Bowl" (Snow), 6

S

salad dressings, *38, 69, 91, 102*
salads, *29, 38, 57, 91, 101-2,*
sandwiches, *16, 20-21, 80*
scarecrows, 94-95; for parties, 15, 27, 36, 55, 66, 77, 87, 99, 111, 130
"Seed Packets" (Husband), 92
septic tank incident, 104-5
Shiitake Mushroom, Baby Beet, and Yellow Pepper Salad, 102
Silver (horse), 40-41
Sliced Tomatoes with Basil Onion Mayonnaise, 57
"sontresuliminateintarianismfinitequarish," 32

"Soul Food" (Husband), 53
"Stargazer Lilies" (Snow), 106
"staring at the shoulder," 50-51
"Still Life with Blue Goblet" (Snow), 118
"Still Life with Hyacinths" (Snow), 63
"Stone Angel" (Snow), 109
Strawberry, Peach, and Plum Shortcake, 59
Sun-Baked Bread with Olive Rosemary Spread, 30
"Sunflowers" (Husband), 58
Sunrise Eggs, 37
Sunrise Service party, 35-36

T

"Tea Service" (Husband), 83
Tea Time party, 75-77
"Tea Time" (Snow), 74
Tomato Aspic with Avocado Mayonnaise, 79-80
Tomato Green Chili Dip, 16
tomato overdose incident, 22
The Tomato Taste-Off party, 13-15
"Tomatoes on the Vine" (Snow), 12
tomatoes, 13, *16, 17, 19, 22*-23, *57, 79, 101, 114, 122*
Top of the Hill Birthday party, 127-30
"Tropical Picnic" (Snow), 33
"Twilight Magic" (Husband), 96

U

The Unexpected for the Expecting party, 85-87

V

vegetable dishes, *17, 19, 20, 29, 56-57, 58, 68-69, 79-80, 89, 91, 100, 113, 114, 123*
Veggie Triplets, 91
Veggie Wraps, 131, 132

W

Warm New Potato Salad, 57
"Washing Tomatoes" (Snow), 21
Watermelon Punch with Fresh Fruit Garnish, 88-89
"Watermelon" (Snow), 137
"Whatta Tomato" (Snow), 23
"Wheelbarrow with Lilacs" (Husband), 7

Y

"Yellow Flowers" (Snow), 67

Z

Zucchini and Yellow Squash Casserole, 58